The Voice of My Boundaries

Life-Changing Exercises Your
Other Coaches Didn't Tell You About

The Voice of My Boundaries

Venita King

The Get Me Thru Collection® presents
The Voice of My Boundaries by Venita King
Huntsville, Alabama 35806

ISBN 0-9723788-3-9

Printed in the United States of America

I OWE AND DEDICATE THIS BOOK TO

my MaDear, Mrs. Carrie Bell Clisby, for making sure I received loving seeds of wisdom and to Mrs. Annie for forcing me to give them nourishment at an early age.

The two of them contributed more to this book than any other person on earth and that includes me. They are responsible for my most memorable Wisdom Episode with *the voice of my boundaries*. They also helped to reveal the universal spirituality of my voice. Their impact on my life is only a portion of their compassionate legacies.

My MaDear's wisdom and compassion was a fortress for her own boundaries. Wisdom obviously protected her from the malice that forced silence in her day. Perhaps that is why the voice of her boundaries also became my cherished inheritance. It is because of her strength that I am able to share the experiences that created this book.

Thank You to MaDear and Mrs. Annie, whose earthen voices are now silent, is merely the initiation of my thanks. Therefore, it is my prayer that this book stands as evidence of my thanks, through the lives touched by **The Voice of My Boundaries.**

A Word of Thanks...

Allow me to thank God for trusting me to experience **The Voice of My Boundaries** and for allowing me to deliver it to you.

"I thank you God for this gift and for making it clear to me that it is an intended blessing for others. Thank you for being The Spirit that embraces and protects my sometimes faltering and challenged spirit. Thank you for sharing your spiritual light. Thank You for allowing each person who believes in your light to use it as a guide for surviving and getting thru. Amen."

CONTENTS

INTRODUCTION

BOUNDARIES DEMAND TO BE HEARD

There will come a time in your life when memories will be your most valuable asset or your greatest liability. Life has taught me to respect the power of memories and to also embrace the power of the boundaries that direct them.

I mentioned Mrs. Annie earlier in the dedication. Mrs. Annie helped me *to see* myself from the inside out. She is also the reason I believe we have the potential to become spiritually immortal through memories. Divinely, some memories never die. Stay with me because this is a sound perspective. We are taught from childhood that each one should teach one. The goal is for all to grow through teaching and sharing. In other words, we are all expected to pass on little pieces of ourselves. Ideally, the productive teaching should never stop. It saddens me to know we live much of our lives blind to the power of the spirit we each share. Somewhere along the way we stopped listening to the boundaries that define us. However, *spiritual boundaries* can never be silenced and of that I am sure. This book is a testament to that certainty.

I am also certain I was born to write this book. However, God required me to live it before delivering it to you. I have learned much about boundaries and have gathered many nuggets of wisdom along the way. Expect blessings from them throughout this book. I assure you spiritual boundaries are lifelines and not just barriers to keep others out. That is a perspective I want to strengthen for the duration of this book. Boundaries are a part of your gift of life. Boundaries prepare you to go out and live with those who desire to come in. *Whew!* Allow me to define boundaries for you. *"Boundaries are standards of life set by your Spiritual DNA. Boundaries act as the internal guide for growth and protection. They are exercised by choice, but are also committed to God to impose consequences when ignored."* Can you see it? Boundaries will encourage you to go out as well as encourage others to come in. They divinely set the standards that all must honor. It is simple, but not easy. Perhaps, that is why I was required to live this book before delivering it. I am committed to making the message of **The Voice of My Boundaries** clear and simple. I ask that you embrace my definition of boundaries and prepare to grow more through it.

The voice of your boundaries will demand its day, either in your heart or in the hearts of others through memories you create. You see, the *little voice* that lives in your soul and not in your head is never apart from your being. When you choose not to listen today, it stands by while you create memories that are destined to remind you of your actions tomorrow.

Our memories represent a special portion of our spirit and as long as human beings exist, our spirit will have the opportunity to live. The lifetimes granted our spirit are like that of the grains of sand by the sea. Therefore, it stands to reason the *inner voice* that directs our being will be heard despite our negligence.

I learned a valuable lesson about the voice of spiritual boundaries and memories from my son. He was at the tender age of four and didn't know he was teaching me. It happened a couple of years after the tragic death of his dad. I was clearing dinner dishes when he came running down the stairs. He shouted without notice, "Mommy, when I get big I'm going to get me a wife and make her have me two babies quick!" Although a bit shaken, I smiled and said, "Okay..." He continued, "Because if she ups and dies on me like daddy did on you, I don't want to be by myself." I was obviously taken aback by his comment, but I also knew I had to respond. I remembered drying my hands slowly to give myself more time to think. I said, "Well, you'll just have to make sure that you create some good memories, because you have no way of knowing how long any one will live." His final comment as he ran back to his room was, "I know, that's why I want them babies quick." I shall never forget that day, as it is a most cherished memory.

My son's comments gave foundation to what I call a *nugget of wisdom.* It blessed me *to see* more clearly the importance of memories and our spiritual boundaries. It was his comments that gave birth to The Get Me Thru Collection® nugget that inspired this introduction.

"We must be careful of the memories we create,
for the day is sure to come
when one of us will be left with them."

GMT 1701

Understandably, memories and the voice of our boundaries are inseparable. The secret is to live life as if you are going to be the one left with the memories, because memories are not easily erased. Mercifully, the one sure way of creating livable memories is to listen to your *inner voice.* It takes practice and that is exactly where the principles shared in **The Voice of My Boundaries** can help. Exercised boundaries will inevitably result in memories, and I can prove it with your help. Answer these two questions.

"Have you ever been without a memory after listening
to your inner voice or after ignoring it?"
and
"Have you ever had an experience with your inner voice that
did not leave you thinking about what happened?"

Never and *No* are the standard responses from most honest people. Therefore, BOUNDARIES AND MEMORIES ARE INSEPARABLE! Please forgive me for shouting, but I wanted to make sure you heard that point. Meanwhile, you can expect your *inner voice* to shout from time to time as well, if it doesn't already.

Everyone one will create lifelong memories and also live with those deposited in their lives by others. Many of them will be happy, satisfying memories, while a great deal of them will be painful, life-draining memories. Throughout it all, it is important to remember that memories are critical to the quest for peace of mind, peacefulness, happiness and success. There is no getting around it, so save your energy.

I believe we can take back an enormous amount of the control we have unknowingly surrendered by neglecting spiritual boundaries. The rewarding question is, "What elements of memories can you control?" Part of the secret can be found in simply respecting your *inner voice*. The *inner voice* I am talking about speaks for your boundaries through your Spiritual DNA. Every one is different, but we share dreams of happiness, health and wealth. Assuredly, Spiritual DNA charts the course of pathways for every journey in life, from start to finish. **The Voice of My Boundaries** and the **Get Me Thru Exercises** it presents were inspired with that in mind.

We must first give careful consideration to identifying personal spiritual boundaries. One thing for sure, I do not want you to confuse your *conscience* with your *inner voice*. A conscience kicks in after you listen to or disregard your inner voice. Honestly, you know when *the voice of your boundaries* speaks and when it is your conscience. I am convinced the voice of our boundaries guides us while the conscience reminds and reacts.

Our conscience typically speaks in response to a memory while our boundaries, as spokesperson, is the author and director of our memories. *Whew!* I have a mural over an exit door in my home with the *nugget of wisdom* I shared earlier. It displays the commitment I made to myself in honor of **The Voice of My Boundaries**. Here it is again. I encourage everyone to read it before they leave my home.

"We must be careful of the memories we create, for the day is sure to come when one of us will be left with them."

GMT #1701

Before we go further, please don't confuse spiritual boundaries with religious boundaries. They are not the same. You seek out religious doctrines, while you are born with your spirituality. The most powerful of the two should be obvious. *Whew!* Believe me, I know the difference from personal experiences. The confusion causes many people to live outside their Spiritual DNA. Thus, they live unhappily with memories that were not embraced by their boundaries.

Our spiritual boundaries stand at the threshold of every memory we create, or should I say, that we allow. I have found it to be interesting how so few people consider the memories they are creating. Perhaps that is why we are left with so many regrettable ones. *There are few memories that will escape a spiritual boundary.* Ponder that simple statement for a moment. I want to inspire your thinking, for we have all been created to become wonderfully different human beings. My point again is, our personal boundaries represent our Spiritual DNA. If not, *How would you describe such individuality in human beings, given they yet seek the same end?* Consider this nugget of wisdom while you ponder.

"No two voices are the same even when they are destined for the same place."

That element of uniqueness is what helps define our peacefulness in success or failure. So you see, it doesn't matter if you are a success or a failure, your spiritual boundaries will always have center stage in your life. Respecting your Spiritual DNA can afford peacefulness in both your successes and failures, and that is the foundation for *getting thru.* Expect to hear more about the *get me thru* journey before you finish reading **The Voice of My Boundaries.**

I encourage you to explore this book as a journey. You will discover *nuggets of wisdom* about becoming your own best friend. You will also find inspirational reinforcement for living beyond surviving. All of these characteristics are necessary to be successful in having your spiritual boundaries work for you instead of against you. You will learn how I came to know my own Spiritual DNA and how I learned *to practice* requiring others to respect it as well. The key word on this page is *practice.* Look for key words like this throughout this book. Also, expect to learn how to strengthen your emotional, physical and financial spirituality, which compels others to respect your boundaries.

I understand it is going to take time to accept the perspective of *Spiritual DNA.* I am therefore going to equip you with points of clarification regarding spiritual boundaries. Chapter Five provides clarification of spiritual boundaries. It reveals experiences of how my own spiritual boundaries demanded and received respect. Chapter Five gives painful details of how *the voice of my boundaries* changed the literal course of my life in 2003.

This book is not just a self-improvement book, but it is my opportunity to coach you using a gift from God. I am going to Coach you into a sincere self-evaluation that will leave you empowered in many ways. Also, I want you to read this book with expectations:

- Expect me to Coach you on every page, listen for my voice through the words as a conversation
- Expect to sift through *nuggets of wisdom* for what fits you
- Expect *to see* yourself as you never have before
- Expect to be challenged like you never have been before
- Expect to consider familiar aspects of life from new perspectives that ignite inspiration and yield wisdom
- Expect to use old words in new ways
- Expect a universal application of spirituality
- Expect this book to be a conversation and not just words
- Expect that your reading this book is just the start...

Any success you experience from reading and working with this book will be the result of action taken by you—nothing more and nothing less. Please don't let this book become another motivational read. It should become your call to action. Let it become what I believe it was meant to be, and that is *an inspired work that changes lives through new practices that generations will embrace and pass on.*

Remember your boundaries have a voice whether you listen or not. The way to grow is to listen to *the voice of your boundaries,* especially in times of challenge. Before you choose not to listen just remember, *the voice of your boundaries* can be unforgiving through its memories. It rarely retreats until you acknowledge it in some form. There is no peace of mind when you fail to listen. Don't ignore it and it won't betray you. Partner with it and don't cause it to use force to be heard. The scars from its demands are most often left as heavy and painful memories.

I am going to use each exercise in **The Voice of My Boundaries** to Coach you into one of the most rewarding partnerships of your life. That is a memory I look forward to sharing with you!

My memory prayer is:

"Lord, should you grant me mercy today and I not die,
please also grant me actions today
that will not cause me to wish I had. Amen."

Allow me to make a clarifying point about my prayers. I will share short prayers with you from time to time. I practice Christianity and my prayers are reflective of my faith. Whatever you do, don't stop reading because of their inclusion, as no one is an island. My prayers help to get me thru and that is why I share them. I am not so arrogant to believe that every aspect of this book is for every reader. Let me assure you now, it is not.

Treat this book as you do other elements of life. In other words, everything that is happening around you does not necessarily affect or apply to you. I have listened to numerous speakers only to leave with a single *nugget of wisdom.* However, the nuggets are still priceless to me. The blessing of *choice* controls the final results anyway. Nevertheless, I am indebted to the power of my faith because it enables me to share my gifts with you in this way. I am committed to their inclusion, because I have also discovered that my memories have the potential of being someone else's lifeline. You just might discover you have a few lifelines of your own to share. You are certain to have a new definition and empowered respect for *the voice of your boundaries* when you finish.

I encourage you to honor your boundaries as if your life depends on them–*because it just might.* I am ready to work with you now, but you must be willing to work more. On that note, let's get started.

CHAPTER ONE

THE CRITICAL MISSING LINK

A matter is critical when it is important to a great majority of people and when it has the potential to drastically change lives. It is therefore safe for me to declare that exercise is high on the critical scale. I am also declaring there is a critical missing link that suspends most exercise programs before they even get started.

You don't have to go far these days to find a tailored-made exercise program. Everywhere you go people are pitching new exercise equipment and new dieting programs. One would expect exercise to be old news, but it is current news everyday. Actually, exercise is one of the hottest niche markets of the 21st century. Thousands of new programs are developed daily. Exercise is also a huge money-maker, because the industry is depending on your never getting it right. Thus far they have not been disappointed. You and I have contributed to the madness through our obsessions for the idealism advertised in marketing exercise. Obsessions are money-makers! I am convinced that most obsessions are unsuccessful searches for the missing link. The deeper you look, the more you *will see* that something is missing or one good exercise program would be enough for everyone. The right exercise program is magical, but the magic is not in the program. The magic is in you. The missing link is the key to revealing the essence of the magic.

Why are we obsessed with exercise these days? Why is every other commercial and infomercial about weight loss, body toning, anti-aging or about some other physical dissatisfaction in need of a miracle drug? The answers are simple—benefits and profits, which by the way are two of the most powerful words on this commerce-driven earth. The other answer is that everyone wants to look good and feel good. The bottom line is, good looks are profitable and often result in other wonderful benefits. That is the whole truth.

Few people will admit it, but we have become fanatical behind the lures of looking good. However, you can't have good looks and a great body without exercising something. The price for it is secondary, and most people will never experience their fantasy. Frankly, millions are living unfulfilled lives because of a failure to connect the critical link with their desires for perfection. Most people are struggling to find a magical place in life called *peacefulness* filled with explosive amounts of happiness that will last them a lifetime. However, packaged fantasies cause many to bypass fulfilling micro moments of happiness. The full euphoric season many people seek rarely happens.

I have discovered that you can actually experience peace of mind, peacefulness and happiness by exercising body and soul. True, such a declaration sounds like another cliché, but it is not. Hold on because we are just getting started. I have learned as a Coach that all people don't see things from the same perspective and that is another critical nugget. My goal is to clear pathways along the way to help you *to see* exactly what I mean. You will need to sharpen your ability *to see* in order to master exercise's missing link. I have no doubt you have found the highway that could lead you to success, but watch your turns.

"Once you are on the highway, your turns and exits determine your destination."

I assure you the missing link is going to inflame muscles that you've ignored for sometime. "How can this be you say?" Easy, because most people unconsciously take it for granted or just ignore it, which is when the pain starts. Take a moment and reflect on the inner strength you knowingly honor and prepare to strengthen it through every page in this book. The mere thought is empowering and I pray you feel that way too. All power begins within before any outward use is possible, which explains why some people seldom win at living life to its fullest.

Actually, this is an excellent time for you to begin painting your own portrait of exercise's critical missing link. My wager is you and I will meet in the middle or at the same conclusion before you finish the Get Me Thru Exercises. Take a moment and answer a few questions. Don't skip them because they are going to help you *to see* the missing link. Answer the questions in the spaces provided, but use a pencil instead of a pen. You will experience some growth as you use this book and some of your answers are going to change. This is *your* book, so don't temper your answers. Your openness will help you to master the exercises later. I guarantee you this is not going to be your typically shelved book. I expect **The Voice of My Boundaries** to become one of your trusted reference books, so don't let me down.

1. What are your strengths? *Here is a tip.*

Strengths are closely aligned with whatever you practice daily. However, my being correct does not necessarily mean you have developed the best strengths for you. There is a chance you could be contributing to your own weaknesses and that is one of the things we are going to discover with the Get Me Thru Exercises. Your weaknesses can actually come from that which you practice daily.

Be sure to catalog that point in your spirit. Your strengths may fall into several categories such as, physical, spiritual, financial, professional, social or more. Be specific and add to it what applies to you.

____
____
____
____
____
____
____
____

2. What is/are the most powerful and dependable sources of your strengths? *Here is a tip.*
My most powerful and dependable sources of strength are prayer and skilled meditation. I have learned to exercise both to my advantage and I practice them daily. There are scores of books to help you and I confess to having purchased my share in a quest for personal fulfillment. I am going to create a Get Me Thru Rolodex soon and list the books and other resources that have helped me. Meanwhile, use my tips and your experiences to respond.

____
____
____
____
____
____
____
____
____

3. Did you expose any weaknesses while identifying your strengths?

Yes______ No ______

One easy way to uncover this answer is to go back to those things you would like to have listed as your strengths, but could not for some reason. Chances are, you will answer *yes* once you review your list of strengths. Here is a tip.

Most people who think they know me will be surprised to learn that my initial response to this question included spiritual and social qualities as my weaknesses. Socially, I have always been one of those people with an uncanny ability to 'rise to the occasion'. You know the kind who never meets strangers and is not afraid to speak up. However, it became an unfulfilled part of my life that I was rarely comfortable carrying out. I was always giving out more than I received, which left me weakened. Spiritually, I felt there was something missing even though I grew up in the church and did not stray away. I was even a faithful attendee throughout college. I wrestled with the doctrine of religion which represented the ideologies of man to me. Conversely, spirituality represented the universal power of greatness for all human beings and not a select few.

I have grown to believe that everyone has the power to be the best they can be through spirituality. I also believe it is a divine quality that surpasses religion. Admittedly, it was also my fellowship with people from all walks of life that changed my perspective about spirituality. Thankfully, I discovered how to separate the doctrine of religion from the spiritual, which revealed the beauty and the power of universal spirituality. Today, spiritual and social qualities are listed as my cherished strengths.

If you answered yes, write down the weaknesses you uncovered. Again, elaborate on what you list. Your answers will help you more than you know right now. It is fine with me if you are not comfortable with the questions. Even so, I expect you to answer them anyway! This is one of those times when you will just have to trust your Coach.

Weaknesses:

Once again I cracked the door for you to siege a glimpse of your spiritual empowerment in the making. Remember, empowerment is not something that is poured on you, but something that you innately possess. An imperative condition is that you must nurture it to experience its benefits. *Empowerment is that special quality in the spirit where you begin to build on greatness bit-by-bit and day-by-day* Whatever you do, don't pass up an opportunity to experience spiritual empowerment.

There is an agenda in every word I write. It is to help you *to see* the power in identifying your spiritual boundaries and listening to your inner voice accordingly. Specifically, I want you to begin looking for wisdom. Wisdom however comes at a price, but go ahead and use it, for I have paid for most of the wisdom shared in this book. You will need to think, think, think and then think some more *to see* it and keep it. You won't gain from this book if you are not a thinker or working on becoming one. I will tell you this much and that is, the missing link was revealed in the introduction. I assure you empowerment will not come through mastering physical exercises only. If so, we would not need as many exercise programs on the market today.

I discovered long ago the critical missing link controls success and that all who neglect it eventually fail. You can not afford to slight it and help is on the way. Some of the most demanding physical exercise programs on the market will be easy once you absorb the new perspectives presented in **The Voice of My Boundaries.** I am convinced of it and I plan to prove it to you.

Now, don't misunderstand me; physical exercise is an awesome conquest. However, you risk putting the cart before the horse without the critical missing link. Don't join the growing list of unfulfilled quitters. Ask yourself, *How many exercise programs did I want to start, but never did? How many exercise programs have I started, but never finished?* Why not? I'll take the witness stand now because I too am guilty. I have spent a small fortune on *the perfect for you* exercise programs. My mistake was I approached each program as the quick fix presented by advertisements . When it wasn't quick and didn't fix the problem, I quit and bought another one. I absolved myself by conceding all the others were wrong for me. Can you believe that? I am happy to report that I have learned how not to quit, so don't despair. I will tell you how to overcome such behavior in Chapter Seven. Once again, the point is something critical was missing.

I am treading lightly in this chapter, because I am aware that most exercise programs are rarely finished. I also know you might quit before getting to the finish line, even with this book. I don't want you to quit. You don't know it yet, so I will tell you that once you finish this book you are just beginning. Beginning is the only way to change something! In the meantime, allow me to plant a seed of wisdom here: Practice using choice as one of your strengths. There is power in *choice,* because it allows you to sleep and it at least stands as evidence of why you can't sleep.

"Choice may not lead you to perfect behavior, but it is certain to afford you wisdom in your consequences."

Okay, back to more proof about my critical missing link perspective. I have observed physical fanatics and I am certain you know a few as well. In fact you might be one yourself. I hope you are, because who better to fill in the blanks in this section? Hard body fanatics exercise in the morning and evening until their bodies resemble that of Mr. and Ms. Universe. They have breathtaking physical appearances and yet you may see little life in their eyes, which reflects their spirit. Their spirit presents them as wanting and lacking. Don't miss the point and wander off, because I gladly concede that not all awesomely developed individuals with hard beautiful bodies are unfulfilled. However, I place the odds against many of them when I consider the one-dimensional focus on the physical. A true exercise program is comprehensive and that is another nugget of wisdom.

Stay with me please, I am not proposing that you stop your physical regime. I am suggesting you add the critical link that will give clarity and balance about the total you. Specifically, clarity on who you want to become and how it can be achieved. I hear you saying, "tell me something new or tell me about it." Believe me, that is my intent and the Get Me Thru Exercises in this book will make it all clear and simple. However, I want you to remember that I did not say it would be easy.

Each Get Me Thru Exercise helped me to recognize the need for changes in my life. They also helped me navigate the steps to mastering the changes. No doubt, the most valuable has been to preserve my changes. Amazingly, **The Voice of My Boundaries** protects me from those who try to stand in the way. I proclaim to you that when you master how to preserve declared change, your chains will release you as well. Afterwards, you will travel pathways that uncover the secrets of living a fulfilled life spiritually, physically and financially. These exercises will guide you all the way.

The exercises in this book are effective partially because they constantly expose the missing link. They are also designed to bring about powerful changes. Unfortunately, if you are not careful, they will also create the problem of how to keep those changes in place. I have just revealed another secret you will need to uncover for yourself as you perform each exercise. The secret is not hidden, but I can't guarantee you that you will *see* it. If you miss it you will not experience success with these exercises. However, I will tell you that a critical clue is fused in the action word *change.* I pray you don't miss it.

Remember, you always have *choice* on your side, because choice is exercised from within and always before exposing your decision to others. You should never accept life without choice, even when others attempt to rob you of it, because that is when your boundaries become your strongest ally. This is where I hope you begin *to see* how critical your spirit is to your getting stronger. Keep reading even if you missed the point, you are certain to understand it as you move into the exercises. Crease the top of the last two pages so you can revisit them later if you feel you did miss the point.

You will soon find that honesty is one of the required characteristics to gain strength through the Get Me Thru Exercises. You must decide to be honest with yourself before attempting even the first exercise. If not, you will surely miss the benefits and profits that having the missing link guarantees. Certainly, you know that even the best guarantees are conditional. Likewise, this guarantee requires that you now make an important decision about your strengths and weaknesses. Don't worry, I'll help you.

First, The Get Me Thru Exercises enabled me *to see* what I call my *needs and the maintenance link*, which involved identifying and addressing my own weaknesses. So, you must also decide if you want to identify your weaknesses. The decision to do so is one of the critical pathways to building strength. *Can you accept being weakened to experience the full measure of your strengths?* Your answer will let you know just how far you are willing to go. It is no easy feat, but winners are doing it as you read.

My first book, **The Get Me Thru Collection®** minibook, reveals an inspiring nugget of wisdom on weaknesses that may influence your answer. Its full meaning is clarified in a later chapter in this book.

"Take more time getting to know your weaknesses and you will spend less time showing them to others."
GMT #1702

I assure you that your weaknesses will become new pathways to more of your strengths once you begin to honor the power within. You can have it all, just not all the time! It is important for you to remember that having it all spiritually, physically and financially requires wisdom borne out of endurance and courage. You cannot afford to forget that you are a part of the society who believes the more physically attractive you are, the greater the opportunities for benefits and financial reward. Please don't expect me to waste your time trying to defend this point. We are clearly a nation driven by physical beauty and wealth.

Once again, an old revelation leads us to more questions. The two new questions are:

How then can more people win considering
the monotonous unconquered challenges in life?
and
How can discovering exercise's missing
link increase the chances of more victories?

We must consider the odds before tackling those questions. The odds are clearly against most of us, unless we master building *muscle through personal spirituality.* Did you get that? How can that be when the spiritual is regarded as an invisible entity?

"Spirituality may be invisible, but the manifestations of spirituality in action are not invisible."

Shamefully, we have much to overcome regarding spirituality and frankly, it will take longer for some than others. You are the only one who honestly knows how much muscle you are willing to build under such circumstances. The circumstances most people are forced to survive will not just disappear. Consequently, that leaves *change* at the doorsteps of many.

I asked you to be honest, and I shall give you nothing less in return. I have concluded that we practice physical fitness and then we pray the spiritual will be ignited somewhere along the way. Please be warned that crimes against peace of mind, peacefulness and happiness are being committed. People are sentencing themselves because of a lack of spiritual resolve of self. I do not mean religious knowledge, but spiritual knowledge of self. One is far more powerful than the other, so please don't get derailed before we begin. Besides, I already gave you my perspective on those differences.

I suggest to you that whatever you wish to possess, you must also plan to strengthen it by using it. Idleness is a breeding ground for a loss of power. That philosophy applies to most things in life. New car engines for example that are rarely ignited will soon lose power. The thoroughbred horse picked to win the Kentucky Derby and only allowed to run at race time, is certain to lose as well. The same applies to our spiritual knowledge and spiritual power. Similarly, I have witnessed people needlessly drowning in self-induced misery because of an unused, weakened and powerless spirit. I believe that I have half of the resolve and I know you possess the most important half, so keep reading.

It is easy to overlook that which is not in immediate sight, but it is more dangerous not knowing to look. Don't forget you were born with the most important secret to overcoming weaknesses and increasing your strengths.

There are many nuggets of wisdom unveiled in **The Voice of My Boundaries**. However, the most effective answers for your life are within you. Remember, you are on the road to extracting the most powerful one of them. I know you hear that all the time. *Look inside yourself for the answers.* It is the truth and truth is what releases freedom and freedom creates choice and opportunities for success. The challenge is learning how to look inside and then what to do afterwards. I asked you earlier to look for clues. Well, I am not only going to give you clues. I am going to give you the answer and here it is.

"Mastering spiritual resolve, which is a universal application of spirituality, is the critical missing link."

I can't say that enough, because the essence of it is clear to me. Spiritual resolve is most critical whenever you accept the challenge of change. Why? – Because we are all unique and our approach towards the same end is likely to be different. That is why I decided to give you the missing link now and a hundred times more before you finish this book. Pause here for a moment, because spiritual resolve is no small matter. Spirituality is universal and not in a box, which makes it difficult *to see* from points of individuality.

Therefore, each exercise in this book is designed to give *the voice of your boundaries* well-deserved privileges to force an exercise of universal spirituality. I am convinced that each Get Me Thru Exercise represents the essence of the spirituality needed for all exercise programs. Incidentally, each Get Me Thru Exercise embodies spirituality in ways to help you fill in the blanks for your own life. Let me also point out that spirituality does have a sense of humor. You will therefore learn *to see* that wisdom releases you to laugh both at and with yourself. I must admit that I almost missed it myself by taking my life too seriously.

Please remember as you consider my perspectives that everyone has a voice representing their boundaries. It is unresolved actions that deafen ears to hearing it. Again, you can read about a very personal experience of mine in Chapter Five, but please don't go there now or you will miss the point I am making now. I assure you it is going to be a revealing chapter. The experience in that chapter opened my spiritual awareness of self-more than I ever imagined. I pray you will also gain from the principles of its revelation.

Completing the exercises in this book will leave you knowing who you are from the inside out. If you practice them, you will also learn how to love yourself better, while exercising with **The Critical Missing Link.**

Henceforth, I am going to be your Coach, and I am expecting you to emerge stronger and a winner more often in life. I am going to encourage you and challenge you. More importantly, I am going to inspire you— expect it to happen.

Let me share one final point. Wisdom is a wonderful breeding ground for confidence, and confidence rarely takes itself too seriously! Each Get Me Thru Exercise is about how to live your life within your spiritual boundaries when life's experiences and others don't seem to know the difference.

Now take a deep breath and let's move forward.

A Get Me Thru Nugget:

"Success without wisdom is only luck,
because wisdom is clearly revealed
and doesn't just happen."

CHAPTER TWO

THE WARM-UP

Warming up before beginning a new exercise program is an act of wisdom, because exercise programs target changes better achieved with preparation. Believe me, you want wisdom on your side with any exercise program. I want you to pause for a moment and give your spirit notice that something is about to happen. You will need support with this book, and this warm-up is an excellent source for support.

Don't forget, you just learned that the critical link is *spiritual resolve, which also means to apply universal spirituality*. Be smart and always partner with your spirit. Few people will have the power to compromise your relationship once spiritual resolve is established. That is a powerful nugget of wisdom.

Warming up the muscles before a new exercise program prepares the muscles for the strenuous demands ahead. Think of this warm-up as a pop-quiz with an open book. Whether you pass or fail, you will have increased your chances of success for the true challenges in life. *Whew!* Always look for support in my italicized words, because they will always reveal elements of encouragement.

As your Coach, I want you to hear my shouts of encouragement and whispers of caution. I want you to grow stronger while you come to grips with your boundaries through these exercises. I want you excited and thankful for each day you are blessed to share your newly exposed gifts with others. I want you to be a vessel where wisdom grows. I want you eagerly seeking challenges that will allow you to achieve your dreams on this side of the Jordan River. I want you prepared to answer my questions, but I also want you prepared to produce more questions of your own. I have discovered that using realism to create questions is more valuable than always having the answers for someone. *Why?* Because questions require that you pause in life. However, always having the answers fed to you presents a spiritually crippling alternative that works against your inner voice. Answers often cause you to stop too soon. *Whew! Will somebody please say Amen!*

"Will somebody please say Amen!" is one of my inspirational clichés which means, *if I stopped here I am leaving enough food for this part of your journey*, so expect it from time to time. Remember, this is a spiritual exercise program designed to make you think. It is my prayer that you are now mentally and spiritually prepared to warm-up from the inside. The outside will follow in time.

Before we move further, it is important for you to accept during these exercises that *surviving* is a precondition to *getting thru* and not the crowning goal. I need you *to see* that *surviving is a state in life's circumstances designed to get you to the next day by any means necessary.* In other words, surviving is not enough! Surviving is the preparatory stage for achieving true success. It only allows you *to see* a glimpse of what you can have after you *get thru.* I want you *to see surviving and getting thru* as the elements in life that will either take you all the way together or leave you standing still. Eventually, one will leave you with wisdom and one will reveal the need for wisdom. Are you getting warm?

Let me share a little more about surviving, because it can ruin your exercise program if you don't have a clear perspective of what it offers. Surviving alone is what causes disrespect of your boundaries when you stay there too long. Surviving alone can become an ally of your spiritual enemy by luring you into states of compromised success. You know exactly what I mean. I am talking about the times when others see you as successful, but you know the whole truth. I am talking about the you they know and the you that only God and you know. Surviving alone makes it easy to slip into such states in life. I need you to accept for the sake of this exercise program, that *surviving* and *getting thru* are co-dependents. You can not win without exercising both. I guarantee you comforting success with your exercises in exchange for accepting this perspective.

I encourage you to read **The Get Me Thru Collection®** minibook if you haven't already. I call it my 92-pages of light. It is *packaged for the pocket and tailored for the soul.* You should be able to finish it during a meditative lavender scented bath. It will help in your warm-up preparation for sure. You will find in it why I strongly subscribe to employing common sense. I believe common sense reflects the inner spirit and is an excellent foundation for wisdom. Besides, common sense works miraculously well when you begin something new. I believe common sense is critical to success in life, even though we also overlook its power. Common sense is powerful, because it often leads to wisdom based questions. Remember my passion for questions and expect many of them along the way. In fact, I will anticipate yours and ask them for you, and of course I will answer most of them as well. Did I hear you say, *What is common sense and what does it have to do with warming-up for exercises?* That is an excellent question and I will be happy to answer it. I believe that *common sense is an embryonic exercise of wisdom.*

• Common sense is a facet of thinking you must have to keep the scientific in a productive perspective.

• Common sense is a facet of thinking that alerts you before you travel miles beyond your destination, even though the map suggests otherwise.

• Common sense is knowing when and when not to take action.

• Common sense is a facet of thinking that focuses on footprints rather than the words only.

• Common sense is education that money cannot buy.

• Common sense is innate Mother wit.

• Common sense is a facet of thinking that encourages total observation over spotlighted participation.

• Common sense is a facet of thinking that allows you to run vicariously with challenges instead of away from them.

• Common sense is a facet of thinking in constant anticipation of wisdom.

• Common sense is a facet of thinking that silently weighs the intents of others.

• Common sense is a facet of thinking that uses listening as a means of tempering the tongue.

• Common sense is a facet of thinking that let's you know every smile does not deserve a follow-up, which clears pathways for the spirit to observe.

• Common sense is a facet of thinking you exercise before deciding to show people how smart you really are.

• Common sense is a facet of thinking that reveals a missing step in the instructions. It tells you to at least look at the picture on the box before spending hours trying to force the pieces or quitting.

• Common sense is a facet of thinking that does not require an exaggeration of one's knowledge as proof.

• Common sense is a facet of thinking that creates fortunes.

• Common sense is a facet of thinking that respects the tongue as a manufacturer of good produce or famine.

• Common sense is a facet of thinking that cautions you to observe the whole room and not just an occupied corner.

• Common sense is a facet of thinking that baffles scientists.

• Common sense is a facet of thinking that allows you to find the right way on roads without signs.

• Common sense is a facet of thinking that helps you *to see* why things received outside your understanding are actually gifts. It also enables you *to see* why gifts deserve thanks that may warrant a lifetime of humbleness.

Okay, I was just testing you with that last one, because I know it actually describes wisdom. Finally, I believe common sense is an internal blessing purposed to help you move beyond surviving. The key is you must reach within to exercise common sense. I hope you get the picture. I assure you that few lazy people are blessed with common sense, because you possess it by doing and not by being slothful. *Are you getting warm yet?* Think back to the last time someone you know was accused of not *exercising* common sense. Did you get that? Exercising implies work and lazy people don't like to work. Lazy people like benefits, but are not willing to pay the price to have them. Did I hear you ask, *Do all lazy people lack common sense?* My answer is, *laziness is enabled by a lack of common sense.* My MaDear constantly cautioned me to avoid lazy people. Her nugget of wisdom:

"Lazy people can get you killed. They cut corners, lie, cheat and steal. Stay away from lazy people!"

Will somebody please say Amen!

Just remember, common sense is an important characteristic when it comes to successful results. The key is to control as much of the results as humanly possible. Common sense plays a vital role in all life's results and I am speaking from a point of wisdom.

Your spiritual muscles should be experiencing a sensation at this point. If so, your warm-up is going according to plan. If not, start over until you begin to feel something special within. You will know when it happens. Remember, everyone has an *inner voice* waiting to guide their common sense. Please let there be no doubt, you must learn to employ common sense everyday if you plan to move beyond surviving. A lack of common sense will keep you standing still without notice. Granted, I said in my first book that **"Sometimes standing still keeps you moving"** and it can, but not in this case.

Nevertheless, I have wonderful news. You are blessed if you know that you do not exercise common sense. However, exercising it is simple; but *you must learn how to listen to hear its voice.* It is not going to be easy, for experience has also shown me that most people void of common sense do not exercise effective listening. Thus they rarely hear what others are saying. Don't anguish over it, because if you are willing to work—help is on the way. I believe we are all born with the spirit to exercise common sense. My challenge is having you *see* the significance of faithfully exercising it. Given my many revelations about common sense, I hope you *see* you can only access its power through your spiritual will. Are you feeling this yet? If so, nod your head. Go ahead no one is looking. If you did nod, consider it a powerful affirmation. If you didn't nod, you should have!

If you are feeling warm at this point, you are either getting it or certainly getting close. Now, let me share another view of common sense from a perspective of surviving and getting thru. I hope you still agree with me that surviving means you just make it to the next day. You don't move beyond your issues because you rarely leave anything behind. You courageously or cowardly make it to the next day. However, when you courageously survive you do so with plans of moving beyond surviving.

Conversely, when you cowardly survive, you simply want *to see* tomorrow's sun and the night's moon—nothing more and nothing less. Roget's thesaurus describes *survive* as, *"to keep the wolf from the door."* Theoretically, the wolf could stalk you as long as he lives or until you take decisive actions to get him away from your door permanently. I am not implying that you should kill him, though it may be your only alternative. However, the wolf will continue to be your nemesis until you exercise some decisive action. You may be the only one who knows the wolf is at the door and that is when the light of your spirit's worthiness shines. You are never alone as long as you exercise your points of spiritual resolve. Perhaps that is why I love it when I see people talking to themselves. Of course, I know not all of them are sane, but you can often and easily make that determination. So, the next time you see someone talking to himself, pause and observe them as inconspicuously as possible. Then pause again *to see* what you really observed them doing. It is quite interesting. Are your muscles feeling this yet? I hope they are feeling warmer.

Regarding the wolf, when he stalks your door you can spend the rest of your life peeking from behind a few barriers and roadblocks, or you can deal squarely with him. The problem with a plan to just survive is you won't know if the wolf is planning on getting thru or just testing your spiritual resolve. The result is clear when only one has a plan to get thru. However, it is up for grabs when both of you have a plan. The truth of the matter is you won't have the choice of never going outside and not seeing the wolf. There is certain to be a time when you will come face-to-face and that is when your inner power will be tested.

Don't forget an important principle of getting thru once you decide to conquer the wolf. Finish it and let the dead bury the dead, so to speak. There is no benefit in carrying dead weight. Why would you want to carry the demised anyway? The peace of the dead is untold and they certainly are not in need of help from the living. The more wolves you carry on your back, the more weight you will have the next time you meet another one. It may be the whole pack the next time and you won't be prepared because you practice just surviving. Get it? I am convinced the TV show "Survivor" reflects my perspective. My point? The objective on the show is to make it to the next show and to be the last one standing in the end. The goal to merely survive means the participants can not afford to look beyond the current day, even with a million dollars at stake.

Whew! Did I just describe you or someone you know? Survivors rarely shed their challenges even after they conquer them. They are programmed to hold on to them. Great survivors are carry-over specialists and seldom experience true happiness or peace of mind. I know, because I was a proud survivor a few years ago.

I wish I had known what my MaDear knew years ago. By the way, you may call your Mother — Mamma or Mommy, but mine was simply *MaDear*. I always saw her as being mine and she is still very dear to me. She survived multiple myeloma cancer far longer than her doctors predicted during late 1970s through 1981. Her survival was during a time when people believed cancer to be contagious or acted as if it were. She lived every day looking for ways to move forward and beyond her cancer. She never denied having cancer; she just refused to give in to it. She was an incredible woman and way ahead of her time. I didn't know that she was planting so many secrets of getting thru in my spirit, but she knew. Actually, I wish we did not refer to those living with cancer as mere survivors, because so many living with cancer know more about getting thru than we ever dreamed. They are champions of cancer—Champions!

Will somebody please say Amen!

Having you accept that surviving is just the beginning is crucial to success with your exercises, so please indulge this warm-up a little more. Chances are, you too are a practicing survivor or you would not be reading this book. Don't despair, because I wrote this book from personal experiences and that should tell you something. Experiences helped me *to see* that one resting in the bosom of surviving can become desensitized to the danger signs. Consequently, life is resigned to the premise, "If I just get up in the morning I'll start over and get back in the race." I ask you:

- *What is going to be your starting position when you get back into the race tomorrow?'*
- *How can this kind of progress be measured? Is there ever-true success for you practicing surviving alone, relying on tomorrow?*
- *Is there enough effective power to live within your spiritual boundaries when to survive is the only goal?*

The answers should have you burning up by now. Grab a towel because we are not finished. I have concluded that few people are immune to the lures of merely surviving. The income level and life-styles run the entire scale. I believe many people live without ever practicing *getting thru.* The result is that many people live hard, fall hard and some even die hard. Surviving can be captivating, so you must be strong to move beyond its lure. **The Voice of My Boundaries** and the **Get Me Thru Exercises** offer a good place to start seeing mere survival in a different perspective. I suggest you concentrate on new perspectives that require an application of universal spirituality, commitment, common sense and a *get me thru* resolve.

Admittedly, surviving and getting thru are not new to life, but they have been overlooked as being the powerful team they were meant to be. I liken them to trust and a promise. It is nearly impossible to experience the fullness of a promise without trust. I challenge you to make it happen without experiencing both. They hold power in their own right. However, they only become powerful after they begin to work together. It is therefore important to remember that others may easily recognize when you are merely surviving. You can become their prey, as it will be clear that your spirit is not being strengthened. They may capitalize on your weaknesses and use your weaknesses against you to advance their own goals and dreams. The Get Me Thru Exercises will help you to recognize them while you are preparing your spirit for growth.

We are all different, so don't expect to complete the exercises as you would a race, because this is not a race. This exercise program is the beginning of accepting new perspectives. It may take a few weeks or several months for you to complete all the exercises. Your success is contingent on your decision to practice the principles of getting thru for the rest of your life. It is important that you decided to start now. I applaud your initiative. Here are the final tips in your warm-up.

• Read the entire book before you begin the exercise program. I need you to strengthen your spirit and sharpen your quality of common sense, inspiration and wisdom. Your reading the entire book will also reveal that honesty is the key to true success. However, you have my permission to stop as instructed on page 53 and complete the Actions for the Peaceful Location in the Mirror Me Thru Exercise.

• Always remember, it is imperative to be honest with yourself first. I know from personal experience and I am not proud of that confession, but it is the truth. It was perhaps one of the most difficult revelations from the exercises for me. I will tell you about it later.

• Don't start your exercise program the same day you finish reading the book.

• Keep a pencil with your book always. As your Coach, I don't want your spirit interrupted by having to look for a pencil. I know it sounds trivial, but it is more important than you know at this point.

• Don't plan to share your book with anyone else. You will be required to make very personal notations in it. You will have time to decide whether you want to share your book later. Be sure to make all the required notations when coached and keep your book secure. Let me caution you that others may not understand some of your transitions, unless they too are working on honoring *the voice of their boundaries.*

Finally, I once thought one of the worst things a person could do was to forget who they are. Now I know, *not to ever know who you are is even worst.* Well, that concludes your warm-up.

A Get Me Thru Nugget:

"Sometimes it is not that you didn't say Thank You, but that you forgot you did."

CHAPTER THREE

THE WORDS OF GET ME THRU

My uncle Charles Hawkins often said to me, *"Dee, say all of your words."* I love words today because of him. His influence and wisdom causes me to focus more on how I deliver them and how others receive them. Uncle Charles believed that understanding came from clarity of speech, which I too accepted. I also accepted that perceived meaning and syntax are equally critical. However, I use old words from an inspired perspective throughout this book. My meaning and syntax may read differently from similar discourses. Therefore, clarifications are necessary. I will not risk having you *see* this as a motivational book only, because it is not. Frankly, that is the last thought I want to leave with you.

Even so, I too have bought and read many books only to finish them feeling as if I missed something. My feelings were worsened if the authors convinced me they had answers to my questions, but didn't deliver them. The secret was in the words and the perspective from which they were delivered. It took many books and even more dollars for me to learn that nugget. I also learned that most inspired writers present their thoughts from gifted perspectives, which means they were writing from places within themselves. Though it was obvious to them, sadly it was not always delivered to the reader. Thus, I like many others were left to personal interpretations and thus resorted to old practices. The goals were obvious, but the essence of the perspectives was clouded by the dependency on tradition.

Meaning is expected to give clarity to one's syntax, which gives a book its life or its demise. I have no desire to create new words; I simply want to use a few old ones differently. Therefore, I have transformed some in the spirit of inspiration, blessings and commitment to **The Voice of My Boundaries.**

You will see that I placed a glossary in the beginning of the book instead of the end. Why?—Because, I ask many questions throughout the book and most of them are about a perspective that has to do with my interpretation of certain words. I realize words are seeds for the spirit, but meaning, application and understanding are what give words fertility. I want to plant a few new seeds and I want them to enter your spirit with opportunity for growth. Having their meaning more accessible is my way of giving you an edge!

Words are powerful, but the spiritual power is supremely embedded in the meaning and use of them. Words are used to encourage, discipline, and to govern lives, but they also destroy lives. Words separate people and bring them together.

It is my prayer that the Get Me Thru perspective of each word enables your spirit *to see* how to be the person you were born to become.

Boundaries: Standards of life set by your Spiritual DNA. Boundaries act as the internal guide for growth and protection. They are exercised by choice, but are also committed to God to impose consequences when ignored.

Champion: A Get Me Thru word for one living with cancer

Change: A life altering practice

Common Sense: Embryonic wisdom delivered through one's spirituality

Conscience: The voice that reacts to your actions

FEAR: **F**aithful **E**xercises **A**cknowledging **R**everence

Financial Wellness: Financial Peace of Mind

Get Me Thru Partner: Someone you trust to know your strengths and weaknesses and your plan of action for living better despite them

Getting Thru: The ability to move beyond surviving to fulfill the *whole of life*

Healing: A gift God placed in the hands and voices of every human being to make a difference, with a warm touch and kind words

Hope: **H**eaven's **O**pportunity for **P**rophesied **E**vents about life

Humble: Being Humble means: You understand that your gifts have everything to do with others and very little to do with you

Inner / Little Voice: The voice that speaks to you before you take action

Inspiration: A spiritual reception of energy that positions the spirit to receive seeds of wisdom

Memorable Episode: Situation from which you learn lessons that remain in your spirit and lead to wisdom

Mere Survival: Making it to the next day by any means necessary

Motivation: The result of calculated experiences for emotional euphoria and it is also a profitable marketing tool

Pausing: An opportunity of quietness to listen in order to hear

Peaceful Location: Special space for meditation and solace

Perspective: A spiritual interpretation of what you *see* through your spirit.

Prayer: Spoken and unspoken communications with God

Questions: Thought provoking words that drive you to actions and to pathways of wisdom

Revelation: A component of wisdom that exposes the right questions through more questions that lead to life-changes answers

Seeds: Daily deposits of nuggets for living that require wisdom for discernment and nourishment for life

Spirit: The supreme essence of *you* revealed through the voice of God, who is universal

Spiritual Resolve: Universally applied spirituality through the voice of your boundaries

Spirituality: Your DNA exercised in response to your divine destiny

Strength: Power that drives you forward from within

To See: Ability to spiritually visualize and process beyond what natural eyes afford

Voice of My Boundaries: The inner voice that speaks as the guardian of your Spiritual DNA

Weaknesses: Power that holds you back from within

Whew!: A soft sound that represents an act of spiritual exhaling

Why?: A powerful question that affords you opportunities of silence when needed and opportunities to be heard when needed

Wisdom: A purposed application of life that God reveals through the spirit of those who seek it

Workshop: A spiritual opportunity to work and shop for *nuggets of wisdom* that are designed for the mind and tailored for soul

A Get Me Thru Nugget:

"People often see who you are through the eyes of their own needs. You cannot afford to rely on their assessment alone—know who you are for yourself."

CHAPTER FOUR

THE MIRROR ME THRU EXERCISE

Welcome to The Mirror Me Thru Exercise. It is unique in three ways: It is your first exercise. It requires reflective patience and it sets the stage for every exercise in this book. It is a prevailing exercise. This exercise also requires a standard of creativity that probably has not been requested of you lately. Therefore, it is important that you follow all the instructions to the best of your ability. The *best of your ability* is an encouraging request, because it erases the fear that causes you to complain or compare. Your best also replaces fear with confidence to set a standard. This exercise is your first opportunity to raise your standard in perspectives and personal growth. I suggest you approach this exercise from the perspective of a wise carpenter who willing measures 2, 3 or even 4 times for one precise cut. Prepare now to add a few things to your physical surroundings and to take some away.

ACTION: A Peaceful Location. A Peaceful Location is your meditation and solace refuge. It is also the guardian of your book, memories, dreams, secrets and peacefulness. It is your perfect place for spiritual nurturing. Everyone deserves such a space and everyone can have one. It may take some thinking and commitment, but it can be done. So, don't start by telling me what you can't do because of this or that. I know as your Coach, you would not be on this field, okay I meant to say, reading this book if you didn't intend to play and win—right? Of course I am right about it. Shortchanging this action will weaken your entire program; so do not take it lightly. I already established mine and I am going to help you establish your new space. Let's get started.

ACTION: Identify and Claim Your Space. Walk through your home and test various locations for comfort and peacefulness. Sit in certain chairs and stand in front of certain windows. Don't force it; if it isn't there, it isn't there. Keep testing until you have that special feeling and then claim it as yours. Make sure it is in a room that will allow you and you alone access at certain times. Notify your family members that you are declaring that particular space off-limits during certain times. Lovingly demand that your request is honored. Now the work is about to begin. This is not going to be an HGTV make-over, but a space tailored just for you. It may require a new coat of paint or rearranging a few pieces of furniture. Don't request the help of others unless you absolutely need their help. Whatever you do, remember our conversation about common sense and don't try to move an armoire by yourself. Remember, this is an opportunity to create some good memories and a space to enjoy and to protect them.

ACTION: Remove the Clutter: Remove all the things that have the potential to become spiritual hijackers. Such things will deafen your ears to the voice of your boundaries before you get started. *Namely, those things that make you feel sad, angry, discouraged, meaningless or unjustifiably confident. This may take some time,* because I am going to ask that you don't just shuffle things around. If there is something in your new space that falls into one of the categories I just described—don't just move it, but get it out of your home. Understand that physical clutter can be just as disruptive to your spirit as it is to the decor of your home. Physical clutter is your number one nemesis at this stage. Clutter is like bad memories and rarely makes room for other things on its own. You must take control and I want to help you keep it. Did I hear you say, "Why is removing clutter so important to this exercise?" That is a fair question. Clutter silently chips away at your desire for spiritual resolve. It is emotionally intrusive and uncomfortable. More importantly, clutter occupies valuable space. Honestly, "How comfortable are you with clutter all around?" Pause on that nugget for a minute. It is important that you make the area yours. Decide now not to settle for less and you won't.

ACTION: Dressing Your Space. Equip your Peaceful Location with special indulgences that make you smile and give you a sense of peacefulness.

My Peaceful Location is in my bedroom. I am fortunate to have a sitting area in it that is calming to my spirit. However, it was just another modest space before I declared it my Peaceful Location. It has a bay window, a small marble top table, a large wooden box, a floor lamp, an oval oriental rug, two wall pictures, a tall green silk tree and an old chair. There is also a small CD stereo player on top of the wooden box.

I set my space up with meditation and peacefulness in mind. I painted my entire bedroom, but I made sure my Peaceful Location was set apart in a special way by using two colors. Now let me describe the items I included in my space and why.

The bay window is a comforting tall three-window layout. It is small yet deep enough to give me a feeling of total separation from the other parts of the bedroom. Size is not the issue, but comfort and peacefulness are, so don't lose your focus because of size.

The table lamp was new and quite elegant. It has faux crackle paint, an ornate pole and a suede swing type lampshade that I absolutely adore. It sits to the right of my chair and the swing shade gives me flexibility for reading.

The small table was already in my bedroom, but in a different location and was previously used as a plant stand. It is a beautiful mahogany table that I bought in a box several years ago. It has a green marble top that needed regluing because of years of use. I have a candle holder and a Get Me Thru coaster on it. I keep my Bible and other books on the bottom shelf. No other items are allowed to remain on the table!

I found the wooden box in my attic where it had been for fifteen years. It was actually used as a shipping crate for a large ceiling fan. Who knew that one-day it would give safe haven to a few of my personal treasures? I stained the box a beautiful red mahogany, but not before sanding it and filling in many nail holes. I keep my final draft of **The Voice of My Boundaries** *and pencil, extra scented candles and a few other special items in the box. Though there is a place for a lock, I have not felt the need to lock it. However, the box and its contents are in my will. A very special person is going to inherit a treasure. I pray their spirit will make room for a few of my memories.*

I mentioned that you might have to rearrange some furniture; the old chair was from my den. A wonderful woman, Mrs. Eveyln Rivers, gave me the chair that adds beauty and solace to my Peaceful Location. I actually grew up with the chair and she always knew I loved it. She gave me the chair about a year before she died. It is in need of covering, but I can't bring myself to cover it. The chair is an inspiring memory that keeps me looking forward. Whew!

The oval shaped rug was already in the bedroom except in another location. It is now difficult for me to imagine it having been anywhere else.

The matching pictures are of flowers that compliment the ambience of the space. I look forward to replacing them one day with pieces of authentic art. The silk tree remained in its original location. It took me approximately two weeks to set up and finish my space, as I was not able to work on it everyday. I hope the tour of my Peaceful Location inspires you to get started and to finish your space.

Don't grow impatient and keep your objective at the forefront of every action. You will know if something is missing. By the way, I added the large wooden box a couple of days after I thought I was finished. Now I can't imagine my space without it. Be careful not to attack this as you would a professional assignment. It is not professional work, but an act of self-love. Set up your space with a spirit of peaceful expectations. Practice setting time aside just for you and then devote that time to creating your location. Remember, most of your actions involve creativity and may require little physical exertion. In other words, creating your Peaceful Location should not be stressful. Keep in mind this is going to become a place where you will afford your spirit rest. I assure you it will give back to you beyond measure. Here is my simple Peaceful Location prayer:

"Lord, please help me to honor my spirit as I prepare and spend time in this special space. Amen."

Stop reading now and clip the top of this page. This is where you will begin reading after you finish setting up your Peaceful Location. Of course, you may go back as needed. I guarantee you will appreciate having your special space. Have a wonderful and fulfilling experience and I will see you in a few days.

Welcome back! I hope you enjoyed designing and setting-up your Peaceful Location. I also hope you meditated on all you have experienced thus far. If so, you are ready to resume, so let's get back to work. By the way, I need you to certify a few items before you continue. Please respond honestly. Actually, I won't know if you lie or tell the truth, but you will. *Whew!*

CHECKLIST:

- ☐ Did you finish setting up your Peaceful Location?
- ☐ Are you pleased with your new space?
- ☐ Have you secured a place for your book and pencil in your location?
- ☐ Are you prepared to be totally honest with yourself?
- ☐ Are you determined *to see* this exercise program to the end?
- ☐ Are you convinced that to survive is just the beginning of getting thru?

If you were able to check each question, sign your name below, for you are ready to continue with a refreshed spirit.

____

Your Signature and Date

Now that you have your own space, sit down and let's have a brief conversation. Chances are you haven't finished the book and that you did stop as I hoped you would to finish your Peaceful Location. Did you stop? Oh well, I am going to proceed as if you did anyway. If I am correct, you now have a comforting place to exercise. You will not perform all of your exercises from your Peaceful Location. However, I trust you will do all of your reading there.

Essentially, the objective of the Mirror Me Thru Exercise is to help you master seeing the real you through the spirit of your own eyes. You have already learned that seeing who you are from the inside out is paramount to getting thru and honoring the voice of your boundaries. This exercise will afford you a first in-depth look. You must know who you are from the inside out to initiate spiritual resolve. More importantly, if you achieve your dreams you must identify for whom you are working, because true achievements are the results of work. Don't pretend this is news, because we already talked about your having to work. I am convinced that someone's plan is always being carried out. Therefore, if you don't have a plan or a dream of your own the sensible conclusion is, you are working on someone else's dream.

Whew! Pause on that nugget for a minute.

This exercise required much of my time and patience. I sought *to see* perfection through it and nearly missed the wisdom. My misunderstanding of imperfection and perfection flew under the radar and blinded me to the importance of their spirituality. This exercise opened a new perspective on an old matter.

"Imperfections should inspire your will to push towards perfection and not weaken your spirit."

Show me a person whose will is strong, and I will show you a person who is in touch with imperfections. This type of person keeps their eyes fixed on perfection and wisdom. This exercise reflects such wisdom like an in-depth mirror. **The Mirror Me Thru Exercise** will give you an aesthetic view from the outside first and then the raw imperfect inside view without any retouching. Your mirror will unveil what it takes to create a beautiful portrait with support from your inner voice. My mirror helped me *to see* I was making an enemy of the voice that was directing my inner strength. Allow me to further set the stage for your next Mirror Me Thru Action.

Looking into your own eyes is going to be difficult and more challenging than meditating. Meditating requires that you clear your head and focus blankly allowing your inner spirit to have its way, healing and ministering to your soul. I don't want you to be blank. I want you to remember everything and everyone you see. The healing and ministering will come later.

You were probably taught as a child to look into a person's eyes for the truth. This exercise is no different from that practice. The eyes have stories we selectively bury. It is for this reason that you must look deeply for yourself. I ask you, Who better to trust? We shall see. Believe me, there are people who know you better than you know yourself. It is because of your spiritually blinded eyes, but that is about to change. Your eyes have been speaking to people on your behalf for years and you thought they didn't know. There will be few secrets as long as there are eyes. I do not believe that secrets are always spoken. However, I do believe secrets are always exposed through the spirit first.

"Your eyes are two of your best friends, because they rarely lie on you and never to you."

Consider how you immediately size up someone after meeting him or her for the first time. Most of the time you were right. You didn't just look at their face or body; you looked right through their very being. You knew within a few minutes if they were sincere or a phony. However, your own eyes are more difficult and besides, it is much easier to look away when no one else is looking. Regarding other people's eyes, you focus on them because you want to know the real person. Guess what? It is not a woman thing. No one and I mean no one can size up another man like a man. I have several male friends from whom I have learned much about how to size-up a man.

This exercise is critical to uncovering your spiritual boundaries and believe me, it is going to be uncomfortable in the beginning. Don't despair because when challenges rise in your life, your spirit stands waiting to defend. Your inner spirit wishes to have a working, compassionate and rewarding relationship with you.

From here I suggest you call a truce with *the voice of your boundaries* and work on restoration for peacefulness.

Remember, if this is your first reading, you won't actually perform this exercise until after you read the entire book. You are reviewing the game plays for now and developing your own strategies.

Relax for a moment and meditate on these questions. They will help to open your spiritual eyes when you stand before the mirror during your Action items.

- Am I as honest as people think I am?
- Am I kinder to others than I am to me?
- Am I seeing the person others see when they *look at* me?
- Do I like the person coming through the mirror?
- What am I seeing that makes me happy?
- Am I where I want to be in my life? If not, why?
- Am I staring at my enemy or my friend?
- Am I surprised by anything *I see* or do not *see*?
- Am I looking solely with my eyes or am I yielding to my inner spirit for truth?
- Can I be trusted to be honest at this stage of the exercise?
- What am I seeing that makes me sad or uncomfortable?
- What am I seeing that makes me content?
- Is there enough respect for the person in the mirror to get thru or just enough to keep surviving?
- Am I as forgiving of myself as I am of others?
- Am I living a lie or am I living the truth?
- Am I *seeing* a person with whom I would enjoy spending the rest of my life?

These are not easy questions and not all of them will apply to you. Granted, you are the only one who knows for sure. There is one thing for sure and that is, most of the questions have significance for most people and that includes me. The questions are to help you focus exclusively on yourself once you are face-to-face with yourself in the mirror. With that in mind, I selected six questions from the group that I want you to answer during this exercise. I guarantee you the answers will become revealing portraits of you and sometimes that can be frightening, humbling and yet spiritually soothing. You should nonetheless experience a release, which is the beginning of the good things to come.

This is a good time for me to share a nugget of wisdom. I am presumptuous enough to believe you have goals and dreams. I also believe one of them is to be successful with this book and its exercises.

"If you are not working on your goal or dream,
you are working on an excuse."
Will Somebody please say Amen!

Please keep that in mind as you work through this exercise and expect me to repeat it. I obviously have no way of knowing when you *get it*, so please indulge my obsession with its meaning. You see, I know life will not stop for any of us to get it. Therefore, we might as well join in and get as much good from it as *possible*. Ultimately, honesty will determine your standard of success with this exercise. There is little growth for you if you can't be honest with you.

I believe Coaches who teach victory through growth should also stand as examples of their philosophy. I offer you nothing less. Accordingly, I included summaries of my six responses as a guide. Again, I realize these questions are not easy to answer. As such, for now I want you to focus on the questions and not necessarily the answers. There is space for your responses at the end of this chapter.

SIX MIRROR ME THRU QUESTIONS:

1. Am I seeing the person others see when they look at me?

I had difficulty with this question and initially my mirror only confused me. I was not certain of what or whom I wanted others *to see.* When this question became important to me I was out of touch with the opinions of others. I was indifferent to people who were not in my inner circle. Yet, I tried to be all things to all people. This question helped me to look for reasons to see the real me. Thankfully, spiritual transitions forced me to accept there is just one me and the opinions of others count as well.

A near-death experience and being called to teach adults in Sunday School are two reasons I am more cognizant of me now. Frankly, a spiritual commitment to my universal spirituality no longer affords me energy to present an image to others that is not the true image of me. I am happier for it, but it was not an easy transition. I must practice it everyday.

This question also brought to light that most of us live for two entities, one life is for us and the other is for those in our lives. I spent the greater portion of my adult life making sure I kept people at a distance without them knowing it. Believe me, it can be done. I mastered it, but it became spiritually draining while creating internal chaos for my body. Internal chaos played a major role in the near death experience I mentioned earlier. I will discuss the significance of that experience later, but for now I trust you have a picture of what this question can reveal.

2. Do I like the person coming through the mirror? Why ?

My answer is Yes, I like the person I see in the mirror today. My Miss Annie Episode prepared me for this question long before I knew there was a need to have an answer. If you remember, I dedicated this book to Miss Annie, but you will never guess why. I overheard her make a devastating remark about my physical appearance. Her painful short statement helped me to focus on people from the inside out and not the reverse. I did not fully comprehend it then, but it had a lasting impact on me. Physical beauty is one of the first things I see when I meet people, but it is not the last thing I remember about them. I focus on seeing how pretty they really had to be in order to be beautiful. You can't see beauty by focusing on the outside alone.

When I look in the mirror today, I see a person who sincerely cares for others and whose faith in God gives her beautiful peace and power. I also see a friend when I look in the mirror. Finally, I see a person who works on living within beauty rather than trying to be pretty. This is not my complete answer, but I hope it helps you.

3. Is there enough respect for the person in the mirror to get thru or just enough to keep surviving?

This question was easy until I considered all three factors together. The real challenge came in addressing the differences between surviving and getting thru. I questioned my state of self-respect once I understood the differences between the two. The fact that I was merely surviving was a difficult admission in the mist of my comfortable success. Nonetheless, I had to face my strategy for success as a coward's way out that nearly cost me my life. You see, I forced my body to store years of stress under the pretense of being strong because no one saw me sweat. Don't judge me yet because I am not alone. This question has the potential to bring powerful images through. Like many others, I was taught never to let people *see* me sweat. Consequently, I did my sweating inside and that can cause leakage and dams and worst. I complicated things out of spiritual ignorance and religion was no help in this matter. *Whew! Can you see it?*

"Sometimes the true complexity about life is in accepting its simplicity."

My first answer was *No.* However, I assure you my answer has changed to *Yes!* I learned the principles of *new perspectives and new practices.* The more I practice getting thru, the more my respect grows. Are you hearing me? Pause here and consider your understanding of surviving and getting thru, and answer as honestly as possible when your turn comes.

4. Am I as forgiving of myself as I am of others?

My initial answer was, "Absolutely not, because I expect more of myself than I do of others." I decided that I could not control others, but I could keep myself in check by holding back certain versions of forgiveness. I now call it my sad version of tough love. It was absent of love, but who knew—Right? *Whew!*

I grew up believing that forgiveness was something you extended to others for a wrong committed against you. Consequently a personal perspective of forgiveness was often unaddressed. It certainly wasn't something openly taught to me. It was also not something you asked anyone else about.

However, my lifetime sentences of not forgiving became noticeable to me. They rarely granted me escape from committed or omitted deeds. I did not hold my head down or go into deep depression or eating binges or anything like that. I did what most strong people do; I kept my feelings inside and just moved them around from place to place with reckless disregard. That can be internally chaotic, believe me. This question revealed a perspective with the potential to kill from the inside out. I was storing an enemy where my spirit lived. In other words, my life sentences turned deaf ears to *the voice of my boundaries.*

I therefore made a list of the things for which I had given myself life sentences. I then made a list of the things I had the power to change. I discovered that I had power over all of them. Ah-ha! Meditate on this question and I pray your revelations are as comforting and spiritually empowering as mine have been. Put your spirit on notice that you want to give your mirror all the help it needs.

5. Am I looking into the mirror solely with my eyes, or am I yielding to my inner spirit for the truth?

My answer was, "I am yielding to my inner spirit for the truth." This question was not a part of the original group I selected. I was therefore farther along in my spiritual journey when I added it to the list. I will share with you that to look through physical eyes is not nearly as challenging. This answer took me into many directions, so I responded with what I call *growth points* courtesy of my spirit. Many of them are the result of what my mirror brought forth through this question.

- I have learned to embrace fleeting seconds of happiness as crowning jewels for my memory chest.
- I look forward to laughter now, when before it was just something I did. There is a difference!
- *I am sorry* or *I was wrong* are not difficult for me to say now.
- I have learned to respect the seasons in every aspect of my life.
- Honesty is more important to me than I imagined.
- I enjoy exercising universal spirituality more today because of my new perspectives and practices.

As far as I have come, everyday reveals enough to me to start a whole new world. My MaDear taught me that nugget of wisdom!

6. Am I a person with whom I would enjoy spending the rest of my life?

My answer was, "Yes I am a person with whom I would enjoy spending the rest of my life." I purposefully looked for positive things, as I knew I would need a foundation for change. I had no problems with this one. Notwithstanding the fact I saw a hard working person in the mirror, who for years had practiced the principles of surviving instead of the principles of get me thru. I saw a decent person in need of much wisdom. I also saw a person who was willing to change. This question was an excellent one from which to build internal power. Essentially, I would enjoy spending the rest of my life with me because I am growing:

- I am slow to take emotional actions based on physical appearances.
- I am loyal to family and friends and that helps me to be more loyal to me.
- I am not as forgiving of my inner circle as I thought. Therefore, I am exercising new practices.
- I am a person who believes there is more to be gained through inspiring a person than there is in motivating only. Motivation needs a constant refueling that inspiration does not. I have grown tremendously from this belief.

Set aside an appropriate amount of time for your Exercise Actions and do not engage in any other behavior while performing them. Clear access to your Peaceful Location with others to prevent being disturbed and turn off the ringer on your telephone. I always take a few deep breaths and meditate before I exercise. If you have a ritual that calms your spirit, make it a part of your exercise program.

ACTION - DAY 1: Stand or sit alone in front of a large mirror with your arms comfortably placed and look into your eyes for as

long as you can. It is going *to see*m like a thousand years, but don't look away. Perform this step at least five times.
TIP: Imagine staring into one of those pictures with the images embedded deeply behind another picture. It requires your unwavering focus *to see* the real image. Only those who stay focused are granted access to the real image. *Whew!* It's true; I bought one of those pictures for my son several years ago. The obvious picture was an ocean landscape of colorful coral. However, the embedded image was a group of flying dolphins over beautiful blue waters. My son and I were able to bring the dolphins front and center. It was indeed an exhilarating feeling. I can't explain how we were able to do it except to say, I know we stayed focused. We wanted *to see* whatever they had hidden in the picture. It was done then and you can do the same thing through your eyes.

ACTION: Retreat to your Peaceful Location, close your eyes and focus on whatever you brought through the mirror. Write down everything you remember and do not consider the relevance. It does not matter if you were thinking about work, the car, your spouse, children, or world affairs, write it down. Do not talk about your exercise, but you may certainly meditate on your entries.
Your Notes:

ACTION - Bonus Option: You may now answer some of the six Mirror Me Thru Questions. The questions and space are at the end of this chapter. If you choose not to at this time, move to the next Action. However, answer them before resuming Day 2 Actions.

ACTION: Secure your book and pencil before you resume your normal activities for the day.

DAY 2: *This stage of the exercise may require a mind over matter attitude to complete, so perform it accordingly. Also, plan to spend at least 45-60 minutes on this part of the exercise.*

ACTION: Stand or sit alone in front of the mirror with your hands comfortably placed and just look into your eyes. Focus on the six Mirror Me Thru questions. I imagine a few of them are still in your mind. Look into your eyes for as long as you can without turning away. If you must turn away, close your eyes and meditate on what you are seeing. Using some of the questions as stepping-stones will help you *to see* the real you.

ACTION: Perform five repetitions of this exercise. Keep in mind you are looking for things beyond the surface.

ACTION: Retreat to your Peaceful Location and make more notes. You may use the responses to your questions to help with your notes. Start whenever you are ready and be specific.
Your Notes:

ACTION: Stay in your Peaceful location for a few minutes with your eyes closed and meditate on what you wrote. Also, think about why you wrote what you did. You may also make any changes now.

ACTION: Read your notes aloud. This is very important. You don't have to scream, just read them aloud and listen as you read. Read your notes as if you are reading the resume of the person who is going to be your partner for the rest of your life. Another point, imagine that as your Coach, I am standing beside you whispering in your ear, *"Are you going to quit because you don't like what you see in the mirror?"* Use the space below to make more notes, especially now that you've had a chance to hear what you said about yourself.

Your Notes:

ACTION - DAY 3: Stand in front of the mirror again and look into your eyes for as long as you can without looking away. It is important that you don't look away. You are doing great and the goal line is near.

ACTION: Retreat to your Peaceful location. Close your eyes for a full fifteen minutes and meditate on all you have seen during this exercise.

ACTION: Write about everything you were able to bring through the mirror. It should be a little easier today. This is not a psychological analysis. My coaching is not about psychology or diagnosing, but about inspiring you. You are painting a self-portrait by collaborating with your spirit. The goal is to capture the real you and nothing more.

Your Notes:

ACTION: Review all of your notes and read them aloud gain. You may also summarize them by days *to see* your inspired revelations. Don't take this part lightly, because it is an important part of your foundation for later.

Congratulations, you have successfully set the stage for *getting thru with your inner voice.* You can step away from this exercise for the next 24 hours. Keep the essence of your notes close to your heart. Doing so will keep your muscles from tightening.

Meanwhile, please allow me to step away to give you a final and passionate glimpse at how powerful the eyes can be for you. My passion for the eyes is because they always have a story and often a humbling one. Strangely, one of my most compelling stories is about a pair of eyes captured in a portrait. I believe this story will bless you by inspiring your spirit to exercise daily.

My husband Robert M. King, a Captain in the United States Army, was tragically killed in an airplane crash in 1985. His remains were not viewable. However, I felt compelled to have his presence represented by more than a gray military coffin. A dear friend, Howard A. Brown agreed to capture Robert's essence on a canvas for his memorial and funeral services. I use the word capture because Howard did not know Robert even though he had met him during military events. I gave him a 5"x7" color photograph of Robert in his military dress uniform. He decided to use pencil because of the pressing time line and I agreed. I became more anxious with each passing day, but I hesitated to interrupt him with telephone calls. I knew he was doing his best to have the portrait finished in time. Nonetheless, my calls to him were always received with kindness, but it was clear to me he was having a problem finishing the portrait. I charged it to his wish for perfection and I assured him it did not have to be perfect. I did not fully understand then how important a role the eyes play in transferring a person's sincere essence. He did finish the portrait in time and it remains one of the most magnificent portraits I have ever seen.

Howard's gifts are too numerous to list and he continues to use them to bless others. I am convinced he stood in God's gift giving line through lunch and recess periods!

However, several months later the story about the eyes was revealed to me. Interestingly, it was not told to me by Howard, but by his wife Betty. I fondly call her Mrs.' B'. The story painted an everlasting portrait in my spirit. I pray you too can see it.

Mrs. 'B' asked me if Howard had talked to me about how difficult it was for him to finish Robert's portrait. My response was, "No, not in any detail." She then with great anxiety told me about the strange experience between Howard and the portrait. Essentially, she awakened one morning around two or three o'clock and realized it was because Howard was not in bed with her. She walked down the hall looking for him. It was about midway that she heard him talking. Her first inclination was to call out to him, but she did not. She quietly paused instead and to her surprise while peeping through a cracked doorway, she watched and listened as Howard talked and pleaded with the unfinished portrait. He was pleading with Robert to tell him about his eyes. She shared that he was begging him for help. Howard, the artist knew the eyes would tell Robert's story and he wanted to capture the whole story. He desperately wanted to give something back for Robert and he wanted it to be truth through his eyes.

Mrs. 'B' said he appealed to the unfinished portrait: "I need your help, please help me to see your eyes. I know they are not right and you are the only one who knows what's missing, do I have them now, is this right...?"

Robert obviously guided him from that point and he finished the portrait while capturing the essence of Robert, the man. Again and without fail, the eyes spoke. Seeing has always been at the center of our being and as you can *see,* sometimes it doesn't matter if the eyes themselves can no longer *see.* The eyes have a story that is visible and that is the essence of having lived. If such an appeal worked through eyes that could no longer *see*, how much more will your eyes reveal to you? *Whew!* Make a strong loving appeal to your eyes for help and then give your inner spirit notice that you are prepared to receive the truth.

YOUR SIX MIRROR ME THRU QUESTIONS:

Do not respond with a *yes or no,* but elaborate. Also, you may skip questions that are uncomfortable now, as other questions may help you *to see* them more clearly.

1. Am I seeing the person others see when they look at me?

2. Do I like the person coming through the mirror? Why ?

3. Is there enough respect for the person in the mirror to get thru or just enough to keep surviving?

4. Am I as forgiving of myself as I am of others?

5. Am I looking into the mirror solely with my eyes, or am I yielding to my inner spirit for the truth?

6. Am I a person with whom I would enjoy spending the rest of my life?

You have just finished learning about how to make **The Mirror Me Thru Exercise** work for you. You can take tomorrow off, but not before taking a few minutes to meditate in your Peaceful Location.

ACTION: Close your eyes and breathe deeply for at least five minutes. Consider this Get Me Thru nugget of wisdom as you meditate.

"The days I dwelled on my failures were days when
I drifted from the spiritual and glanced
into the mirror of man."
GMT #3706

ACTION: Secure your book and pencil and have a fulfilling Get Me Thru Day.

A Get Me Thru Nugget:

"I know I am in trouble when I find myself concentrating on how to deceive me."

GMT #2714

CHAPTER FIVE

AN EXERCISE OF SPIRITUAL BOUNDARIES

An Exercise of Spiritual Boundaries is a story I share with heartfelt feelings. My wish was to share its wisdom only. However, I learned through it that wisdom follows a person's story. Humbled, I conceded that wisdom cannot be seen when it is set apart from a story. The choice to include this very personal story was mine, but the decision to have such wisdom shared was not. Clearly, the wisdom in this story was a gift to me from God and thus a blessing for you.

There is only one Action for you in this exercise. However, it is an exercise from which to gather many nuggets of wisdom. Also, look closely and you will find several empowering principles for honoring *the voice of your boundaries.*

I introduced you to my story about words in Chapter Three. As you know, I have great respect for the power of words. There are so many from which to choose and getting them right is a constant challenge. That was never truer than in writing this chapter. Consider there were thousands of new words added to the Oxford dictionary in August of 2003 alone. Add them to the millions that exist and there is no surprise why our use of them is often misunderstood. God forbid that I share such an intimate story and fail to get the words right, as my ambivalence abounds.

With that in mind, I was inspired to read this chapter to a dear person. I needed *to see* if she would hear the wisdom in the story or focus on the sensationalism of the experience. You see, I also believe words are meant to be melodious and when they are right, readers hear them and keep them like songs in their hearts. Her comments convinced me that she did *hear* the wisdom in the story. She blessed me with this statement, *"You are such a private person and I can't believe that you were so open."* What happened after that convinced me that including this chapter was not an alternative after all. My comment was, "How could I not include it? It represents the essence of **The Voice of My Boundaries.**" On the other hand, the revelation of my remark was in what I did not say, which was *Neither can I. Whew!*

I hope you *see* why my choice of words is critical to prevent sensationalism from overshadowing the inherent wisdom of the exercise. Admittedly, the challenge of writing this chapter nearly caused me to disregard my trusted inner voice. All the more, I am prepared to share **An Exercise of Spiritual Boundaries** with you now. You have my permission to let your guard down, and relax. This experience is a critical part of my journey with the voice that forms my life.

First, it is safe to say that listening to your inner voice is not easy and it is most certainly not an expeditious process. Instead, it falls into the category of being easier said than done. Therefore, view this personal exercise as an opportunity *to see* the cause and effect of spiritual boundaries in action.

My preparation for this exercise began many years ago in my formative years of learning. During this time, I was taught to be Christ-like, loving and forgiving, smart, confident and to stand-up for myself. I practiced perfecting those qualities and I am still trying to get it right. Along the way, I became an unforgiving person and caused many of my formative qualities to suffer. I practiced forgiveness, but with a twist designed to safely absolve me of any wrongdoing. As a child, I convinced myself that being conditionally forgiving was acceptable. It was acceptable as long as my reactions to those who wronged me were not vindictive or harsh. My elementary approach was simple. I would gradually eliminate certain individuals from my emotional circle. Believe me, children are amazing at blocking others out. However, I mastered it so well because I practiced a unique form of forgiveness.

My strategy was to move people away by slowly treating them as if they did not exist. It was easy for me to do as a child. We did not have many material things, so certain levels of dependency were rarely a factor. The people factor was not as easy, but neither was it difficult. Small town living was almost always an assurance of having plenty of cousins and friends around. I could weave in and out so quickly only the truly wise knew that they had been replaced. When physical separation was impossible, I employed my emotional separation strategy. It is incredible what you can train yourself to do as a child. I wasn't afraid to think and take action, even then. Some children are taught fear, but it wasn't taught to me. I wasn't afraid to protect myself and that was how I viewed life at that impressionable stage. I am a formidable life strategist today as a result of the wisdom from those practices.

My thought process however, as a child was *black and white*. It was either right or it was wrong. I don't think I was ever a *gray matter* child. I learned how to take what the wrongdoer said at face value only. I would check and double check to assure myself of protection against a repeat of lies, betrayal and the like. The truth is I would eliminate them from my life when given the opportunity. I can remember not speaking to a family member for several years because I was convinced I could no longer trust her. I would smile or nod, but that was about it. It didn't matter how hard she tried. Once I had given all I was going to give I was out of there and it was normally swift. However, I was true to my early philosophy, which was not to be vindictive or harsh. I was an example of *nice nasty*. People would walk away from me knowing something wasn't right, but they could never put their finger on it. Also, I was always respectful and polite which made it more difficult.

Consider this, my late Aunt Maggie and Uncle Charles loved me dearly. In fact, I was their favorite. Aunt Maggie was not my favorite aunt, but Uncle Charles was unquestionably my favorite uncle. They lived comfortably by standards set during my childhood. He worked in the steel factory and his only son was already an adult and living in California when I was born. They always shared with my family. However, my Aunt Maggie always reminded me of her benevolence. She had a way of making gift-giving look very unattractive. In fact, she made gift giving look ugly. I grew to despise seeing her bearing gifts. I understood her abuse of power over me, even as a child.

Consequently, I did not visit my Aunt Maggie unless my MaDear compelled me to do so. Mostly, my compelling visits included having to clean her house, which I did not mind. She paid me a whole five-dollars for a full weekend of hard work. I often told my MaDear that Aunt Maggie worked me like I was a slave. Even so, I was a good worker, but she was a better taskmaster. She was obviously high on my list for emotional temperament and physical separation.

Nonetheless, my Uncle Charles often made-up for Aunt Maggie's shortcomings and was never a part of my emotional separation. I included him in my life at every opportunity. He had an easy comforting spirit. Once he gave you something or did something for you nothing else was ever said. Uncle Charles encouraged me to speak in complete sentences and to always pronounce all the words. Remember him in Chapter Three? –*"Dee, say all of your words."* Uncle Charles was a gentle teacher who taught principles I yet employ. On the other hand, Aunt Maggie is responsible for my learning how to say, "No thank you." I could say it in such a way that she would beg me to take her gifts, but I would still say, "No thank you." I learned how to respectfully acknowledge and then bypass her attempts to get closer to me. I was *nice nasty* at its best. *Whew!*

Little did I know, my MaDear had been observing me all those years. I told you she was a wise woman who was ahead of her time. However, I thought my actions were justified, since I made no attempt to hurt Aunt Maggie or anyone else for that matter. As a matter of fact, I simply removed future opportunities for my declared adversaries to hurt me. Somewhere along the way my MaDear's wisdom revealed more than my foolish actions alone ever allowed.

I shared with you earlier MaDear died of cancer, which also meant she spent many days in bed. We talked a lot during those times and the more we talked the more I began *to hear* her wisdom. Our conversations were so enlightening. Then one day she turned the table on me. She became less than her usual upbeat self-and said to me, "DeAtri, I worry about you." I knew she was serious, because she only called me by my middle name when it was a serious matter. She talked about her cancer and repeated she wasn't going to be with me much longer. *Whew!* She also made me aware of the contents of her will and requested a couple of promises from me. After that she lowered the boom! I later realized she had carefully chosen that moment. The setting was perfect, only the two of us, and a spiritual quietness that only our old house with its tin roof could afford.

However, MaDear's statement of concern was still hanging in the air, so I responded hoping to put her at ease. I said, "Oh MaDear, you don't have to worry about me, because I will always be able to take care of myself. I have a Master's degree and I am not afraid of hard work. I'll be fine." I thought, *now let's move on to something else.* Only a few seconds passed and then she responded, "I am not talking about that." My God I thought, *What else could you be talking about?* She was obviously reading my expression and quickly replied, "You are not forgiving and that is killing me." How could that be, I thought it was the cancer. Needlessly to say, I was shocked and her words broke my heart. I was living to make her happy and proud and she knew that better than anyone. I remember staring at her in painful disbelief, while her expression remained one of deep loving concern. I was clueless, so much for a Master's degree. *Can you see me?* I sat looking into MaDear's eyes while she faced her own death, only *to see* her using her precious energy trying to save me from acts of a living death. *Whew!*

"Will somebody please say Amen!"

Again, I attempted to put her at ease thinking she just did not understand. I began to present my philosophy of black and white, pure and simple. I told her I did forgive people and that I never tried to get back at those who mistreat me by hurting them. Instead I said, "I just treat them as if they are dead." I actually said that to my MaDear thinking it would help her *to see* my point. She held her head down and softly said, "I know and that is what I want you to change." I said, "MaDear, how can that be wrong if I'm not hurting anyone?" This time her voice was barely above a whisper, "You are hurting yourself and that hurts me." *Whew, what wisdom!* I was twenty-six years old when she opened my eyes to that priceless revelation.

My MaDear asked me to promise her that I would change. Of course I promised her and I have changed. I did so not knowing the principles of *change* would soon become my spiritual ally. My MaDear died a few months after that, but not before compelling me make room for *the voice of my boundaries*.

My reaction to MaDear's request for a change was over-the-top. I forgave people who had no plans of asking to be forgiven. I offered forgiveness to those who didn't ask for it quick enough. I forgave many times in anticipation and to my personal detriment. I was void of the wisdom that only the inner voice provides.

I knew something was missing because my so-called good deeds of forgiving had become emotionally, physically and financially draining. My reformed and forgiving spirit left me in states of incompleteness. My forgiving was a dependable revolving door. It was as if everyone knew I was the *energized forgiver* that would keep on *giving*. My forgiving clearly had been with personal and spiritual disregard. Thankfully, I began *to see* wisdom despite a misguided perspective of forgiving. I sought balance in forgiving and that is when I starting respecting my inner voice. However, it was the revelation on forgiving that changed my direction. Consider this nugget of wisdom.

"Acts of forgiving are not life sentences to personal depletion."
Whew! Did you get that?

My over-the-top approach was not what my MaDear intended. She only wanted me *to see* the internal harm I was imposing on myself by not understanding the difference. Whether individuals remained in my life was not nearly as important as my spiritual neglect. My not knowing the difference was an unhealthy practice pure and simple. Accepting and applying the revelation was comforting to my spirit.

I increased my spiritual study and began to put my newly discovered lessons into action. I was no longer the energized forgiver without a spiritual perspective. My spiritual boundaries guided me before and after acts of forgiveness. As such, I worked hard on developing a relationship with my inner voice. I had no doubt my MaDear was acting as my internal spiritual therapist preparing me to allow my voice to take over. It worked. I sought wisdom with a renewed spirit that brought my voice closer and closer.

Today, I rarely misuse forgiveness nor do I allow it to abuse me. My wisdom-based perspective has never required that I abandon or compromise my spiritual resolve. The transition has taken me from being a righteous unforgiver to fanatical forgiver and finally to an enriched forgiver. Each transition guided me closer to the voice of the boundaries that made the final portion of this chapter possible.

Essentially, my enriched forgiveness helped me *to see* the foundation on which we base our lives is very important. It wasn't just important for me, but it was life-changing. My enriched perspective on forgiveness introduced me to what I call a *foundation principle*. I incorporated the foundation principle conceding that forgiving would always play a central role in my life. This critical incorporation made it obvious that firm foundations are necessary to withstand insurmountable odds. I now yield to the *voice of my boundaries* allowing it to inspect the foundations of my relationships and decisions. Similarly, it clears pathways on my journey that allow me to move forward wisely.

On that note, allow me step away for a moment and clarify a belief about the voice of our boundaries. I believe that it exists for many reasons and we are blessed by two of them everyday.

Provide Protection:

To protect implies that something stands between you and another. Its supreme purpose is to keep your enemy outside. This is made available through the unconditional gifts of grace and mercy. Now I ask you, "If there is something within you and its sole purpose is to protect you, wouldn't you at least listen?"

Promote Growth: To promote growth is that hedge that surrounds you and allows you to work among your enemy without being destroyed. Your listening to and hearing your inner voice ignites inspiration that feeds this growth. Its purpose remains despite your decisions to disregard its presence. Succinctly, no ignition, no growth, but it is always available to you.

Understandably, my commitment to the foundation of personal and intimate relationships is firm. My choices have been carefully thought out and evaluated accordingly. Honesty in personal relationships tops the list, but after that I have proven to be flexible. I believe honesty eventually leads you to the doors you need to open. Likewise, I discovered that dishonesty also leads you to those same doors.

Having said that, I found myself at a good place in life and decided to open a new door after being a widow for nearly sixteen years. I started by reviewing my standards. Of course, my mate had to be a Christian, honest, a good friend first, smart and a hard worker. Honestly, I was in need of few material things. As such, the man I eventually married was one of my dearest friends. I believed him to be honest, a Christian, smart and a hard working man.

I wanted our wedding day to be a fellowship of families and not just a ceremony. We were married on my back lawn and it was all I had hoped it would be. We quickly began working on building our lives together. It was a challenge for him considering he gave up having season tickets for professional basketball and football for small town fun. Nonetheless, he graciously acclimated himself. I did some acclimating myself and it worked out for us both.

He traveled a lot and worked hard. His desire to provide for me was obvious, but he also wanted me to know he intended to care for me even after death. He proved it one day by presenting me with a sizable insurance policy. His enthusiasm about the policy made it obvious he was proud to present it to me. The policy did not excite me, because I knew all to well what needed to happen to benefit from being named beneficiary of one. He asked me to secure it, which I did. He departed for a business trip shortly after giving me the policy.

Soon after his departure I spotted a similar looking policy on top of his garbage basket. I immediately thought, *how did that get there?* I clearly recognized the cover because I was licensed with the insurance company that provided the policy. Of course, I picked it up after seeing his name. Remember I said earlier that both honesty and dishonesty eventually lead you to doors you will need to open? That garbage basket was one of those doors. I opened the policy and began to read it. It was not the policy he had given me and I was relieved. However, curiosity prevailed and I read the entire policy. The beneficiary section troubled me. I recognized his mother's name and his sister's name, but I did not recognize his ex-wife's name. I was aware of his two previous wives, but not the name that was staring back at me.

Surprisingly, I was only concerned and not alarmed. I walked away thinking the policy was reflective of his ex-wife's given name and not the name I was told by him. I went about my day and then my inner voice began to speak to me. I was lead to review the policy once more. This time I focused on the dates instead of names. The dates did cause great concern. I therefore sought to ease my troubled mind by requesting a copy of the public record. I succeeded after a careful Internet search. I used information from the policy to complete the on-line inquiry. It took a day for me to receive the response. Boom! There it was, confirmation of a marriage that had been withheld from me. My first question like any other sane person was, *"Why?"*

Let me step away for a moment. Just in case you can't see it, we are making a full circle back to the implicit wisdom on forgiving that MaDear taught me in the beginning.

He was not there for me to ask him "Why?" and I was not going to confront him over the telephone. I waited, but I did

something else during that time. I felt used and deceived and foolish. More importantly, I felt robbed of *choice.* Having no choice is tantamount to slavery and that is not a recently acquired philosophy. I said things to myself like:
"You fool, how could you not have known?" —"I can't believe you didn't ask if he had anymore ex-wives — as if I thought having two wasn't enough." —"I thought we were friends, why did he lie to me?" — "What is it so bad that he feels he could not tell me?"

The one emotion I did not experience was embarrassment, because I believe embarrassment is self-imposed. With that in mind, I saved myself from some of the agony sure to come.

However, as blessings would have it, I did not stay in that emotional slump for long. I soon began to focus on me. I increased my skilled meditations for relaxation, drank plenty of distilled water, and ate fresh and whole foods. I also exercised and consumed my daily nutritional supplements. I was determined to minimize my storage of stress, as I was certain I would have to address it on a daily basis for a while. It is a good practice to take care of those who take care of you. There was doubt in my mind that my body had proven to be faithful even when I wasn't.

I had two weeks before his return to contemplate my actions, but I took longer. I learned to wait on my voice during uncertainty. I am not sure how long I waited. I can honestly say I have learned that when in doubt, *stand still.* In that instance, **Sometimes Standing Still Keeps You Moving** was an appropriate nugget of wisdom. It was a lifeline I gladly welcomed into my spirit every day. All withstanding, I never once doubted my spirit—never. I sensed the seeds planted by my MaDear were in bloom.

After considerable prayer, I began to revisit our relationship. One, he was my friend and he was otherwise a good man. By the way, I did not tell anyone about what I discovered until much later. I recalled something my MaDear told me after I married my deceased husband, Robert. The essence of her conversation was, it would not be wise to tell her about every little disagreement and disappointment between us. I asked her, "Why?" Lovingly and with wisdom in her heart she said, "Because I won't be able to forget it as quickly as you will forgive him." *Whew!* I immediately grasped her wisdom. Likewise, I wanted to afford my new spouse the same respect. Besides, it seemed logical considering I had not even decided on how to approach him with my information.

Then it happened, *the voice of my boundaries* began speaking loudly to me. It helped me *to see* the cause and effect of choice from an inspired perspective. The revelation required me to revisit what I call *voices of our spiritual being,* namely Conscience, Inner Voice, Little Voice, and the Voice of Our Boundaries.

Conscience: Typically speaks to you after your actions
Inner Voice: Speaks to you before and during your actions
Little Voice: Another way of describing your Inner Voice.
Voice of Your Boundaries: Typically speaks to you at all times and it speaks for your Spiritual DNA.

Someone asked me once, "How do you know if it is the voice of your boundaries and not the devil?" I love that question and here is my response. "How do you know when God is speaking to you?" I assure you that uncertainty is a clear sign that it is not God speaking to you. In other words, to recognize His voice is to know Him. Do you recognize the voices of those closest to you? Chances are, their voices are distinguished and not often confused with the voices of other people. Each voice is divinely unique. Do you get it? YOUR SPIRITUAL DNA IS YOUR VOICE! Okay, I was shouting, but did you hear me anyway? I can't tell you if it is your conscience, inner voice or the whole of your spiritual voice, because I am not you. You and your God are the only ones who will ever know. The question for you to answer is,

"Who put it there?" Most people have difficulty conversing with a stranger about personal matters, so the answer is critical.

Whew! Can you see this point?

I can guide you through my inspired resources, but you will have to do some meaningful work before the answer is ever clear to you. Whatever you do, don't fall for the madness that motivation will get you there. That is like buying swamp land and being excited about building your mansion there. Incidentally, my Spiritual DNA is at work throughout this book.

Meanwhile and during the manifesting of more wisdom, I was guided back to the importance of choice in my decision to remarry. The fact that choice was purposely withheld from me was the focal point. I discovered that our foundation for marriage had suffered severe cracks because of *choice*. Also, the cracks were clearly erosive. It became obvious to me that choice was critical to establishing a firm foundation. Having said that, why then was I having a problem making a decision about how to approach him with my discovery? Easily, because the minute I faced the infectious nature of having no choice my conscience took over and nearly drained the life out of me. It wasn't long before I found myself crossing dangerously into self-resentment. It was not a good place for me.

Whew! Do you see what's unfolding here?

The *voice of my boundaries* prevailed and opened the door that allowed me to recover. I accepted that practicing self-resentment would make it extremely difficult to cultivate self-respect and love. In fact, it can break you down. **The Get Me Thru Collection®** nugget of wisdom below helped me to grasp the essence of what my voice was saying.

"When we fail to love ourselves,
we quickly look to those closest by to hate."
GMT #1709

It was obvious that I was headed in that direction and I was the closest one! My decision had the potential to set me up for the rest of my life. I was determined not to let that happened. Besides, I did not want to hate myself or anyone else. *Whew!*

I called my husband, who once again was away on a business trip. I told him I had some concerns and that we needed to talk. My first inclination was to go to him and have the discussion, but I waited. Once again while waiting, I used the Internet for my research. I knew little about divorce and even less about annulment. I spent the next several days reading. I then called a legal service and presented my questions. It was then that I was forced to address the grounds of devastating choices. On doing so, I was also informed of the grounds for an annulment. I never knew annulment was a possibility. On that note, let me step away again and share another very important point.

Remember I told you how I discovered the facts about my husband's other ex-wife? Well, there is one other detail that I did not share, but I will now. Somewhere along the way and following one of his trips I did ask him about the ex-wife on the insurance policy. I was soaking in a soothing tub of lavender scented water. I knew I needed a special ministering to my spirit and a lavender bath does that for me. I said, "Who is______?" He replied, "I don't know." I had mispronounced her name. He pronounced her name correctly after a short exchange of verbal maneuvering. I added, "Is she one of your ex-wives." He replied a simple, "Yes". The next question was a no-brainer, "Why didn't you tell me?" I was greeted with a cool calm, "You never asked." I am not painting a villainous portrait of him, because he is not a villain. He is still a friend.

The conversation soon took a strange course and led me into unanticipated waters. I closed my eyes and prepared to listen to him, determined to hear his side. Shockingly, he began to talk about another ex-wife of whom I had no knowledge. I quickly sat up in the tub and leaned over to make sure I heard him correctly, as he was in the bedroom. I interrupted him after confirming he was describing someone other than the ex-wife I saw on the policy. I responded, "So, are you saying that I am wife number 5?" He solemnly replied, "Yes." Whew! I had nothing more to add to that discussion and he chose to add nothing more. Thereafter, we both were left to our own spiritual voices.

Now, let's go back to my research and spiritual resolve. The powerful revelations from *the voice of my boundaries* pointed me towards dissolving the marriage. However, there were two conditions. First, I was to perform a specific exercise. Second, dissolving the marriage was to be contingent on my experiencing a specific result from the exercise. Disappointingly, I thought the work had been done. I had no idea the most challenging work was ahead of me.

The exercise required that I return to the principles of having a firm foundation, except with a twist. This time I had to take the pitfalls of deception with me as well. It was otherwise a simple exercise, but not easy and time-consuming. Essentially, I was to travel back from the point of my husband's deception. Specifically, it meant I had to go back until I reached the point of truth in our relationship. Once there, I was to decide if the remaining foundation was strong enough to carry the marriage forward. *Whew!* I did just that and it required a tremendous amount of reflective meditation. I peeled back layers of love, truths; fun filled days, respect, omissions, and lies. In the end, I found myself standing at the door of friendship. My spirit found peace of mind at that door and that is where I was lead to remain. Prayerfully and through wisdom I was able to make the full circle of my MaDear's wisdom on forgiving.

Interestingly though, it was another response from my husband that sealed my spiritual resolve and determined the result. It happened during a sincere conversation. All guards were down when he responded to one of my "Why?" questions with this statement: "I knew you were a sincere Christian and I felt if you ever found out, you would forgive me and we could go on from there." Of course I was going to forgive him, but can you see this picture? His response made it unambiguously clear to me that he had purposely chosen to reserve the *blessing of choice* for himself only.

"How could he have gotten that so wrong, considering Christianity itself is a matter of choice?"

There is no question that Christianity required my forgiveness. Yet, Christianity is not a matter of convenience to comfort or enable deceptive behavior. It is also not a faith of perfection, but one that allows and encourages our living toward perfection. My husband's statement was a clear example of when the right answer is used to provide a haven for deceptive practices. The right question always stands above the right answer. The most powerful question was, *"Is there enough foundation remaining to carry this marriage? My answer was, "No, there is not enough foundation to carry this marriage."* He never asked me that question, but the *voice of my boundaries* required me to ask it.

My MaDear and *the voice of my boundaries* were ever present. They made sure that I exercised wisdom regarding the principles of forgiving and the pitfalls of deception:

PRINCIPLES OF FORGIVING

- Forgiving is not a punitive sentence.
- Forgiving is an act of cleansing.
- Forgiving is an opportunity for restoration or beginnings.
- Forgiving is spiritually ordained.
- Forgiving is divinely designed to move people forward.
- Forgiving affords choice and wisdom.

PITFALLS OF DECEPTION

- Deception can be punitive.
- Deception prevents cleansing.

- Deception blocks restoration and beginnings.
- Deception is contrary to that which is spiritually ordained.
- Deception eventually divides and causes people to stand still.
- Deception attempts to rob you of choice and wisdom.

In the end, my marriage was annulled in July 2003. My ex-husband and I are still friends. In fact, he says that I am the only one of his five ex-wives with whom he has a civil relationship. Please indulge one more affirming point about spiritual resolve.

The day I received my official copy of the final annulment decree was extremely stressful. I therefore sought emotional relief. I decided to go to a movie and then enjoy lunch at one of my favorite restaurants. Unfortunately, an overlooked business commitment only allowed me time for lunch. As usual, I had my small writing pad with me to capture any *nuggets of wisdom* God had for me. I wasn't seated one full minute before my inner voice spoke, "I have a new title for your book." I rarely questioned my voice, but this was an exception. You see, this book already had a title and a brilliant cover, or so I thought. Shocked and completely out of character, I responded aloud, "What do you mean?" That does not happen often! Nonetheless, I opened the cover of my pad and picked up my pencil. The voice angelically said, "The new title is, **The Voice of My Boundaries**. *Whew!* I then replied softly, "Thank You God." The essence of everything that happened to me and especially my writing, evolved full circle from that point. It was a part of my destiny and of course I thanked God for my Spiritual DNA. I ate my lunch in total tranquillity and then cried all the way home.

I need to further clarify why I believe this experience was a part of my destiny and therefore required of me. Allow me to step away for a moment.

I was thirty-two years old when I met and stood face-to-face with my biological father. It was a beautiful California day and I was at peace about meeting him. I stood in his doorway as he stared at me, while saying nothing. I am not sure if he was shocked or if I suddenly became his mirror. Finally he said, "Life is one big stage and we all have a role to play. My role was to help create you." That statement was his only other magical contribution to my life. However, he was right! **The Voice of My Boundaries** *was produced, directed and released through my being a mere cast member on life's huge stage.*

As such, the experience with my ex-husband traveled through my spirit as a baby navigates the birth canal—painfully first and then with a burst of joy! The Director shouted, "That's a wrap" and then gave me a renewed spirit to share my experience with you.

Can you also see how my MaDear's wisdom and this revelation brought me full circle in understanding forgiveness and the voice of my spiritual boundaries? This experience was a tour of **An Exercise of Spiritual Boundaries** through new perspectives. It is my prayer that few others will have to paint such a portrait of themselves. I also pray that my portrait is enough for you *to see* how critical it is to listen to the voice of your boundaries.

Just in case you are wondering, "Do I believe my ex-husband is sorry for his deceit?" My answer is, "Yes, I do believe he is sorry and so am I." Did I hear you also ask, "Why didn't *the voice of my boundaries* speak to me before I married him?" *I never said that it didn't...*

ACTION: Make notes here if you are inspired to do so. If not, secure your book and pencil. Take a few deep breaths and prepare to resume your exercises tomorrow.

Your Notes:

____

____

____

____

____

____

____

CHAPTER SIX

BECOMING YOU EXERCISE

Welcome back! **An Exercise of Spiritual Boundaries** was written to inspire you with more nuggets of wisdom. I have failed miserably if you did not gain from its inclusion. Even so, success with this exercise will require you to use many nuggets of wisdom. Why?–Because you are just pages from setting the foundation for your own exercises of spiritual boundaries. I suggest you begin highlighting nuggets of wisdom that inspired you. It would be wise to consider each as a building block for your foundation.

If by chance you did not take The Mirror Me Thru Exercise seriously, please pause here and go back to complete it. You risk compromising your foundation if you continue. If you did take it seriously, the Becoming You Exercise will not be difficult, but revealing.

The objective of this exercise is to create an actual model of the person revealed through **The Mirror Me Exercise** and the **Becoming You Exercise**. Using the results from the two will reveal no truer picture of you. This point is important, because if you did not combine them you might never know that you were in conflict with you or even better, in harmony with you. *Whew!*

This particular exercise is full of questions, so get prepared to pause and experience a multitude of emotions. I believe questions are one of the most powerful tools available for personal growth. Questions have a way of resting in your spirit when answers can be fleeting. Questions cause you to consider things that otherwise did not matter. Questions create time for opportunities while most answers rush to eliminate them. Questions reveal wisdom without having the answers. Questions are powerful. You will see clarifications of these declarations throughout the exercise.

You will also find a Becoming You Model and assessment guidelines at the end of the chapter. Your answers will ultimately affect the outcome of your model. It is impossible to have a perfect model, so relax and answer honestly. I bravely included my own model for you as an example.

Your questions fall into three simple categories. Namely, **Top**, **Middle**, and **Bottom**. Each category includes causes of life exclusive to becoming you. I encourage you to treat this as an open book exercise and to use your notes from The Mirror Me Thru Exercise if necessary. Also, practice pausing before answering each question and allow the nuggets of wisdom to help you.

You will be happy to know the questions offer multiple choices, but several have follow-up questions. Read each question carefully, as every answer represents a piece of your spiritual resolve for your model. You will use your answers as an artist uses paint when you perform the final part of the exercise.

ACTION: Spend the next two to three days answering all the questions in this chapter. Remember your final instructions are at the end of the chapter. Also, do not answer the questions until you finish reading the entire book!

BECOMING YOU QUESTIONS:

1. Assign a numerical value to each characteristic and your total must equal 100%. **Category**__________

A.____**Common Sense**
B.____ **Being Intellectual**
C.____ **Weaknesses**
D.____ **Strengths**

Explain why you assigned your highest value.

____
____
____
____

Explain why you assigned your lowest value.

____
____
____
____

2. Which do you believe is most effective for change? **Category**___________ Defend your answer.

A.____ **Motivation**
B.____ **Inspiration**
C.____ **Knowledge**
D.____ **Influence**
E.____ **Time**

____
____
____
____
____
____

3. What valuable nugget of wisdom did you learn during **The Mirror Me Thru Exercise?** **Category**___________

____

____

____

____

____

4. Have you ever made a distinction between your ability to *listen* and your ability to *hear?* **Category**___________

A.____Yes
B.____ No
C.____There is No Difference
D.____Never Considered It

5. Which is more important to you? **Category**___________

A.____Hearing
B.____Listening
C.____Never Considered It

Why did you select your answer? Be sure to give one example to support your answer.

____

____

____

____

____

____

6. Which requires more from you? **Category**___________

A.____Hearing **B.____Listening**

C.____Same

7. Will the person closest to you say you *hear* better or that you *listen* better? **Category___________**

A.___ Hear **B.____Listen**

Are you sure? If so, on what did you base your answer?

____

____

____

____

____

8. Is there anyone in your life who would *see* the same person who came through to you during **The Mirror Me Thru Exercise?** **Category___________**

A.____No **B.____Yes**

C.____Not Sure

9. Does your physical appearance match your inner spirit? **Category___________**

A.____Yes **B.____No** **C.____Never Considered It**

10. Did the spirit of who you really are come through during your first exercise? **Category___________**

A.____Yes **B.____No** **C.____Not sure**

11. Do you speak openly about your inner spirit to anyone? **Category___________**

A.____Often **B._____Rarely**
C.____Never **D._____Sometimes**

12. Which has greater power over you? **Category___________**

A.____ Inner Spirit **C. ____Intellectual Knowledge**
B.____Opinions of Others **D.____Never Considered It**

13. Do you feel others are influenced by your inner spirit?
Category___________
A.____Yes **C.____Sometimes**
B.____ No **D.____Rarely** **D.____ Not Sure**

14. Would you recognize yourself if you heard *the voice of your own boundaries* describing you?
Category___________
A.____Yes
B.____No
C.____Not sure

15. To which are you most often responsive?
Category___________
A.____Conscience
B.____Voice of My Boundaries
C.____Inner Voice / Little Voice
D.____Never Considered It

16. How often do you actually listen to your inner voice before making decisions? **Category___________**
A.____Always **C.____ Sometimes**
B.____Rarely **D.____Never**

17. Do you believe your *inner voice* is an actual reflection of who you were born to become? **Category___________**
A.____Yes **B.____No** **C. ____ Not Sure**

18. Are you on track to becoming the person of your dreams?
Category___________
A.____Yes **B.____Not Sure** **C.____No**

19. Do you have a dream that makes you smile?
Category___________
A.____Yes **B.____No**

20. Does your spirit cause you to be *a leader* or *a follower?*
Category___________
A.____**Leader**
B.____ **Follower**
C.____**A Little of Both**

21. If the blood flowing through your body was synonymous with how true you are to the person in the mirror, would you experience longevity or would you die much to soon?
Category___________
A.____**Longevity**
B.____**Live, but Unwholesomely**
C.____**Die Much to Soon**

22. When someone is describing something to you and they say, *"can you see it?"* –what is typically your response?
Category___________
A.____**No**
B.____**Yes**
C.____**Never Considered It**

23. In your words, what does it mean when someone says, *"Do you see it?"* Please do not confuse this with, *"You know what I mean?"* The two questions are worlds apart.
Category___________

____
____
____
____
____
____

24. Classify the following characteristics as they apply. You may assign more than one classification. Example: #4 could be G and D. **Category**___________

CLASSIFICATIONS:

A. Sounds Exactly Like Me
B. No One I Know
C. Most of My Professional Associates
D. Sounds Like My Best Friend
E. Someone I Would Like to Know
F. Sounds Like My Family
G. Sounds Like the Person I Want to Become

CHARACTERISTICS

1. ______Exemplifies control over his/her tongue
2. ______Brings secrets and also takes secrets away
3. ______Deceptive, ruthless and successful
4. ______Humble, gracious, and successful
5. ______Exemplifies spiritual peacefulness
6. ______Rarely smile or speaks kindly of others
7. ______Drains your spirit, rarely attempts to replenish it
8. ______Lazy and a liar
9. ______Negative and miserable
10. ______Overweight and unhealthy
11. ______No spiritual direction
12. ______Has no idea of their inner beauty
13. ______Excellent role model
14. ______Unhealthy due to life-style
15. ______Practices healthy life-style
16. ______Racist, bigot and filled with hate
17. ______ Kind, forgiving and filled with love
18. ______ Self sacrificing to a fault
19. ______ Trust and integrity mean absolutely nothing
20. ______ The world should know them
21. ______ I owe them an apology
22. ______ They owe me an apology

How many?: **A's____** **B's____** **C's___** **D's___**
E's____ **F's____** **G's___**

How have your associations affected who you are becoming?

____
____
____
____

25. Do you find in conversations, you ask your listeners *"Do you see it?"* or *"Can you see it?"*

Category___________

A.____Often **B.____Sometimes** **C.____Never**

26. Have you made a promise recently that you did not keep? Do you believe it is ever to late to keep a promise?

Category___________

A.____Yes **B.____No** **C. ____ See Below**

____
____
____
____

27. Have you stopped in the middle of a conversation and closed your eyes after a forgotten point? If so, why did you do that? **Category___________**

A.____Yes **B.____No**

____
____
____
____
____
____

28. Why do you think I italicized the words *see* and *to see* throughout this book? **Category__________**

A.____Don't Have a Clue

B.____Because:

____

____

____

____

____

____

29. Which voice best describes the driving force behind your thoughts and actions? **Category__________**

A.____Conscience

B.____Inner Voice / Little Voice

C.____Voice of My Boundaries

D.____Never Considered It

30. Do you believe you must *listen first or hear first before* really understanding a challenging point? **Category__________**

A.____Listen B.____Hear C.____Never Considered It

31. How good is your spiritual hearing? **Category__________**

A.____ Excellent

B.____ Fair

C.____ Good

D.____ Poor

E.____ Deaf

32. Which best describes your health? Indicate if it is due to lifestyle or other. **Category__________**

A.____Excellent _____ Lifestyle ____ Other

C.____Good _____ Lifestyle ____ Other

B.____Fair _____ Lifestyle ____ Other

D.____Poor _____ Lifestyle ____ Other

33. When did you discover the difference between *listening* and *hearing?* **Category___________**

A.____Childhood
C.____Adulthood
B.____Don't Remember
D.____There is No Difference

34. Which is easier, exercising your strengths or exercising your weaknesses ? **Category___________**

A.____Strengths
B.____Weaknesses
C.____Never Considered It

35. What did you rely on to complete **The Mirror Me Thru Exercise?** Is it something that you normally rely on in challenging times? **Category___________**

____

____

____

____

____

____

36. Prioritize your concerns. **Category___________**

A.____Yesterday's mistakes
B.____ Tomorrow's mistakes
C.____ Today's mistakes
D.____ Never Considered It

37. Which ability would you like to strengthen in your life? **Category___________**

A.____ Listening **B.____ Hearing** **C.____ Both**

38. How do you let others know they did not hear your point? **Category___________**

A.____Repeat it
B.____ Say, "Forget it!"
C.____Give More Details
D.____Walk off thinking, "How stupid or dumb can you be..."

39. Are you impatient with others who don't readily hear what you are saying? **Category___________**

A.____Rarely
B.______Yes
C.____No
D.______Never Considered It

40. Who do you believe deserves the greater respect? **Category___________**

A.____Person Granting Forgiveness
B.____Person Asking For Forgiveness
C.____Both Equally
D.____Never Considered It

41. Which do you believe is more important? **Category___________**

A.____The Right Answer
B._____The Right Question

42. What question(s) would you like to ask someone at this very moment that could help change a certain course in your life? The course does not have to be dramatic, but should be meaningful. **Category___________**

____
____
____
____
____
____

43. Regarding question #42, is it possible or the appropriate time to ask the person your question?
Category___________

A.____**Yes** **B.**____**No** **C.**____ **I Am Not Ready**

44. Do you sleep well during the night? Do you know why?
Category___________
A.____**Yes** **B.**___**No** **A.**___ **Yes** **B.**____ **No**

45. Do you believe what comes up to your mouth should come out of your mouth? **Category**___________
A.____**Yes**
B.____ **Sometimes**
C.____**No**
D.____**No, but I Exercise Little Control Over It**

46. My mouth does gets me into trouble, but more often for:
Category___________
A.____**What I Say**
B.____**What I Don't Say**
C.____**How I Say It**
D.____**To Whom I Say It**

47. Actions speaks louder than words...? **Category**_________

A.____**No** **B.**____ **Yes**

48. Which makes it easier for you *to see* and *to hear?*
Category___________
A.____**Actions**
B.____**No Action**
C.____**Pausing and Meditating**
D.____**Never Considered It**

49. Which describes you best?
Category___________
A.____Practice Universal Spirituality
B.____Financial Peace of Mind
C.____Professionally Successful
D.____Personal Peace of Mind

50. "I know immediately when I have chosen to use the wrong words." **Category___________**
A.____Yes **B.____No**

51. What is one of the questions you've constantly asked yourself for the past several years?
Category___________

____

____

____

____

____

____

52. Regarding question #51, did the question cause you to experience: **Category___________**
A.____Guilt
B.____Peace
C.____Indifference
D.____Never Considered It

53. Which is more important to you? **Category___________**
A.____ Inner Spirit
B.____ Outer Beauty

54. Can you be trusted? If so, why do your friends ask you not to tell anyone their secrets? **Category___________**

A.____Yes **B.____No**

___

___

___

55. Which means more to you? **Category___________**

A.____To Be Loved By Others
B.____To Be Respected By Others
C.____To Be Liked By Others
D.____Never Considered It

56. Do you conscientiously take care of your heart, the organ? **Category___________**

A.____Yes **B._____Not Very Well**
C.____Working On It **D._____No**

57. What practices do you employ to keep your heart healthy? **Category____________**

___

___

___

___

___

___

58. Hate and hatred are basically the same. **Category___________**

A.____Yes **B._____No**
C.____Not sure **D._____Never Considered It**

59. Which is more difficult? **Category_____________**

A.____To Identify Personal Weaknesses
B.____Others to Know Personal Weaknesses
C.____To Exercise Personal Weaknesses
D.____Never Considered It

60. Which is more important to you? **Category___________**

A.____Health **B.____ Professional Success**

C.____Family **D.____ Spirituality**

61. Which do you devote the most time and concern? The answer does not have to be the same answer you selected in question #60. **Category___________**

A.____Health

B.____Professional Success

C.____Family

D.____Spirituality

62. What causes you to change your direction most often ? **Category___________**

A.____My Own Revelations

B.____Input From Others

C.____Rarely Change My Mind

D.____Never Considered It

63. Is there one particular thing you would change about where you are in your life, especially if you were assured you really could? **Category___________**

A.____Yes **B.____No**

What would you change?

____

____

____

____

64. Regarding question #63, is there any reason why you haven't made the change? **Category___________**

A.____Yes **B.___No**

C.____ Afraid **D.____ Opportunity**

65. Which do you believe is seen more often by others, your:
Category___________
A.____Inner Spirit
B.____Outer Beauty

66. Which would you rather people see first and remember?
Category___________
A._____Outer Beauty
B._____ Inner Beauty
Why?

____

____

____

____

____

67. God has required that you turn your body in for a Mid-Term Lease Check-up. Check all that apply.
Category___________
A.____Excessive Mileage – Lifestyle
B.____Excellent Maintenance
C.____Repairs Needed
D.____Rescheduled The Appointment

68. Do you have a daily regime for maintaining your body?
Category___________
A.____Yes
B.____ No

69. Do you apply the spring cleaning or pruning philosophy to your inner spirit? **Category___________**
A.____Yes
B.____No
C.____Never Considered It

70. Which do you maintain best? **Category___________**

A.____ Home
B.____ Automobile
C.____ Health
D.____ Relationships

71. What is your understanding of the value in pruning?
Category___________

____

____

____

____

____

72. Have you written down your goals and dreams recently?
Category___________

A.____Yes **B.______No**
C.____Going to... **C.______Never Considered It**

73. Regarding question #**72**, if you answered *yes*, write down the accomplishment of which you are the most pleased?
Category___________

____

____

____

____

74. Regarding question #**72**, if you answered no, write down the goal or dream you wished you could have written down.
Category___________

____

____

____

____

75. Do you believe there is an advantage to writing your goals down? **Category**__________

A.____ **Yes** **B.**____**No** **C.**____ **Sometimes**

76. Thus far, which question has been the most challenging for you to answer? **Category**__________

Question #_______

You had to know this question was coming—Why was the question especially challenging?

____

____

____

____

77. Would your best friend say they are pleased with the way you are treating their friend—who is you?

Category__________

A.____**Yes** **B.**____ **No**

Defend your answer:

Step away with me for a moment: I have a couple of dear friends to whom I have expressed my dissatisfaction about the way they treat my dearest friends. They laughed initially, but now they know I have serious concerns. I simply said, "I don't like the way you treat my friend." Of course, their response was "Who?" My answer was, "You!" It gave me an opportunity to open the door for some powerful rhetorical questions. I wanted to leave them thinking. I would say things like, "You treat me better than you treat yourself. Surely, you don't love me more than you love yourself, so why?" "Does it bother you that your actions are hurting me?" Please feel free to add more questions if it will help you to answer more honestly.

____

____

____

____

78. How can you determine when your *standing still* is keeping you moving or causing you to miss out?
Category__________

____
____
____
____

79. Who is the person whom you trust the most and why?
Category__________

____
____
____
____

80. Do you forgive easily? **Category**__________

A.____**Yes**
B.____**No**
C.____**Depends**
D.____**Getting Better**

81. Regarding question #79, would that person be surprised by your responses to the questions in this chapter?
Category__________

A.____**Yes**
B.____**No**
C.____**Not Sure**

If you answered *yes* or *not sure*, list the questions by their numbers that you think would most likely surprise them.
Category__________
Questions: ____ ____ ____ ____ ____

82. How often do you rely on your faith for answers?
Category___________
A.____Rarely
B.____Always
C.____Sometimes
D.____Never

83. Are you a person who practices: **Category___________**
A.____Surviving Only
B.____Getting Thru
C.____Never Considered It
D.____Both

84. Do you ask for forgiveness easily? **Category___________**
A.____Yes
B.____No
C.____Depends
D.____Getting Better

85. Have you initiated any changes since you started reading this book? **Category___________**
A.____Yes **B._____No** **C.____Thinking About It**

86. Is there anything you can do today that will change the outlook for another person? **Category___________**
A.____Yes **B._____No**
What is the logical follow-up question here?

____

____

____

87. If reading **The Voice of My Boundaries** has caused you to rethink a perspective on something, pause now and meditate on it. **Category___________**

88. Who is the person with whom you would share all of your answers? **Category**___________

____

89. Regarding your goals and dreams, do you...?
Category___________
A.____Constantly Complain About Them
B.____Make Excuses
C.____Rarely Achieve Them
D.____Set A Standard

90. Do you find you often repeat the same mistakes or learn from them? **Category**___________
A.____Repeat
B.____Learn From Them
C.____Both

91. From which do you gain the most wisdom?
Category___________
A.____Own Mistakes
B.____Mistakes of Others
C.____Neither
D.____Never Considered It

92. Wisdom means: **Category**___________

____

____

____

93. Would you be happy having you as your best friend?
Category___________
A.___Yes
B.___No
C.___Not Sure

94. What is the kindest thing anyone has ever done for you?
Category___________

____

____

____

95. Regarding question **#94,** who knew first, you or the person who extended the act of kindness? **Category**___________

A.____**I Knew First**
B.____**The Person Knew First**
C.____**Not sure**

96. Do you resist change even when it is to your advantage?
Category___________

A.____**Yes** **B.**___ **No**

97. When it comes to having some time alone:
Category___________

A.____**Rarely an Opportunity** **B.**____**Whenever Possible**
C.____**A Must** **D.**____**Working On It**

98. Regarding *Your Peaceful Location*, what has been the advantage in having your own space?

____

____

____

____

____

99. Would you say you arc as loyal and honest with your self as you are with your very best friend on earth?
Category___________

A.____**Yes** **B.**____**No**
C.____**Sometimes** **D.**____**Never Considered It**

100. List 3-5 qualities you believe every genuine friendship or relationship needs in order to establish a solid foundation? **Category**____________

1.
2.
3.
4.
5.

Regarding your answer to question #100, list the qualities that are applicable to the foundation you've established with *the voice of your boundaries*?

Category____________

1.
2.
3.
4.
5.

Coach's Tip: You can learn a lot about a person through the company they keep. Question #24 is about the company you keep. Be sure to assess it honestly and correctly.

Your Becoming You Model

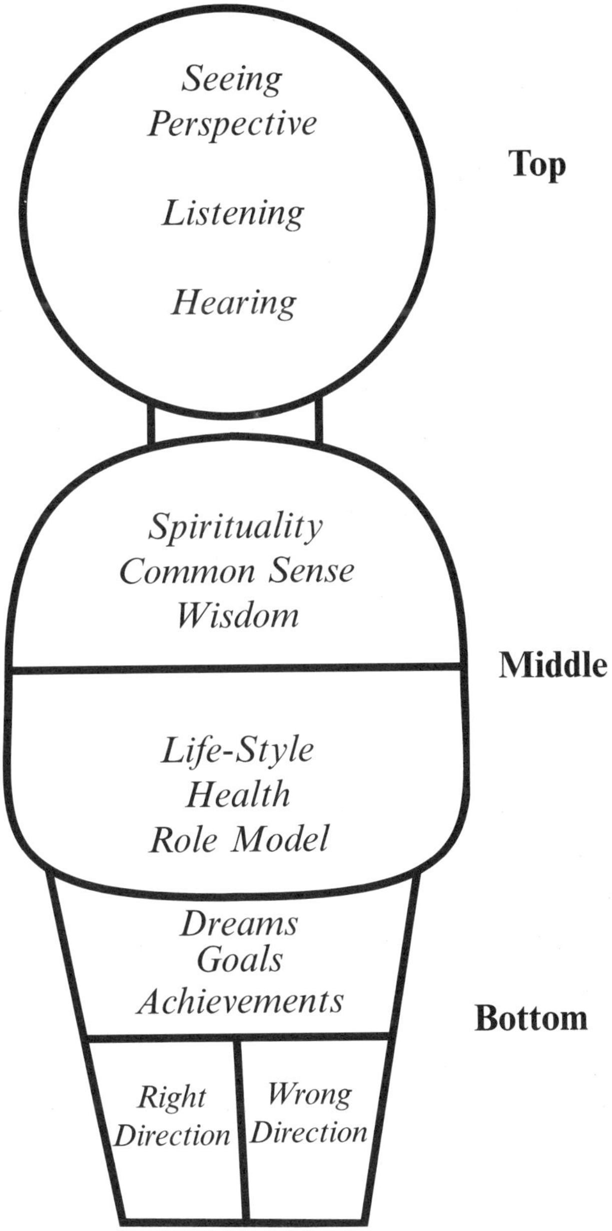

Congratulations on completing **The Becoming You** questions! More importantly, I hope you were honest. If you were and focused on the questions, you have nothing to worry about. Nevertheless, you should have experienced at least one *Aha Moment!* There is a problem if you did not, which means you are probably having second thoughts about specific questions. This is a good time to go back if you are and revisit those questions.

Surely you want *to see* your score now, but just a score would be too easy. There is no score; instead you are going to use your answers to create an inspired model of yourself. Follow the assessment guide and I hope your self portrait is revealing.

BECOMING YOU MODEL ASSESSMENT

ACTION: Study the Becoming You Model on page 117 very carefully. Focus on the characteristics in each category. I suggest you study them one category at a time. Concentrate on what each one means to you.

ACTION: Read each question again and assign each one to a specific category, Top, Middle or Bottom when you actually perform the exercise. Use the space titled Category that follows each question.

Here is an example using Question #56.

"Do you conscientiously take care of you heart, the organ?
Category: <u>Middle</u>

A._X_Yes	**B.____ No**
C.____ Working On It	**D.____ Not Very Well**

This question clearly falls in the Middle of the model, but your answer actually determines if you gain any shading credit toward your model. If you are a smoker and do not exercise, and do not practice healthy eating, you should not gain any credit from this

question. I am not a smoker, I do exercise and I practice healthy eating. Therefore, I gained credit toward shading in that area.

I believe your returning to the questions will help. However, if you are comfortable with your honesty and understand the application of the characteristics, you may disregard categorizing the questions and move to the next Action.

ACTION: Use your affirming answers as an artist would use paint and shade your model on page 117 accordingly. Do not consider an answer totally positive if it revealed something is missing or lacking. Be sure to view my personal model on page 120.

ACTION: Answer one final question after you complete your model. Does your finished model look like you?

A.____Yes

B.____No

C.____Some

D.____Not at all

ACTION: Take a few deep breaths and be sure to secure your book and pencil when you are finished.

Venita's Becoming You Model

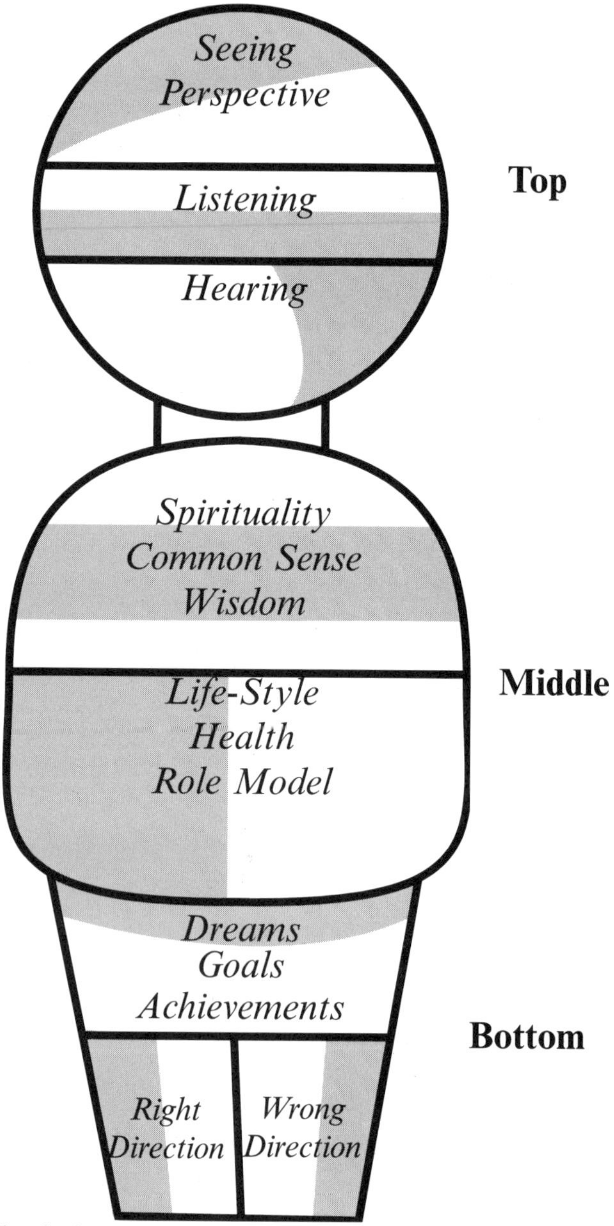

My unshaded areas are important to me. However, I now practice universal spirituality. I therefore focus on the *whole of life* instead of symptoms only.

CHAPTER SEVEN

EXERCISING WEAKNESSES

Thus far, you have experienced a unique warm-up, some old words from new perspectives and three revealing exercises. The first exercise introduced you to a Get Me Thru perspective that only your personal reflection could reveal. The second one allowed you a vicarious experience through an intimate exercise of my spiritual boundaries. Finally, a third exercise guided you in creating a self-portrait from visual and spiritual perspectives. However, this exercise is designed to help you identify and exercise your weaknesses. I will coach you until you become stronger through them and despite them.

Weaknesses are powerful and should not be taken lightly. Wise people choose to exercise their own weaknesses without being forced. I realize exercising weaknesses is not a common perspective to accept. However, I assure you that your weaknesses and mine are exercised everyday with and without our permission. Exercising is just not your normal description for it. Remember, everything about **The Voice of My Boundaries** focuses on a Get

Me Thru perspective. Exercising weaknesses offers a perspective that demands new considerations. Don't fear your weaknesses, because you just finished setting up a good foundation in Chapters Four and Six.

Consider this, I believe there are two types of weaknesses that are vital to success in life.

Type 1: Self-Imposed Weaknesses – Weaknesses created because of something you knowingly did or did not do. Issues from birth do not fit into this type, because you did not create your birth. You were the birth! Allowing such inclusions would be unfair and potentially crippling. The kinds of weaknesses that keep you standing still are yours to have or not to have and are self-imposed. Granted, many self-imposed weaknesses could follow a trail of legitimized excuses, but that is not a part of the perspective. Clearly, if you imposed the weakness, you can also exercise it to reverse its impact on your life. Can you see it? I am coaching you to think and not to hand-feed you.

Don't just read, but follow me thinking! Self-imposed weaknesses are also practiced consistently, which allows you to comfortably blame others for their power over you. How you ask?—Great question. Easily, when you knowingly fail to exercise your weaknesses you are vulnerable and you become open prey to observers. You then settle on the excuses for your failure as observers advance through your weaknesses. *Whew!* Did I hear you say, "Give me an example?" My pleasure. Procrastination is an excellent example of a Type 1 Weakness. Procrastinators are masterful at delaying action or not taking it and then blaming those who move forward for their failure. Procrastinators are the worst, because their self-imposed weaknesses causes them to get farther behind while adding to the excuses. Procrastinators practice exercising excuse building instead of exercising their weaknesses. They postpone matters long enough for a legitimate excuse to surface.

Self-imposed weaknesses are very dangerous. They can fly under the radar through denials enabled by welcomed excuses all the way to failure.

Type 2: Forced Weaknesses— Calculated weaknesses designed to break your spirit. These too are dangerous, but for different reasons. Forced weaknesses are placed on you by others as stumbling blocks and out of fear of your potential. Little can be done to prevent this type, but much can be done to minimize the impact and reverse it, giving you back control. However, Type 2 Weaknesses are obvious as they leave a void if your eyes are open. Did I hear you say, "Give me an example?" It is my pleasure again. Consider when you are robbed of the opportunity to be prepared, but you are still required to compete. The competition could be anything and the reason for denial could as well. The facts are what are important. Fact: You want to compete. Fact: Preparation is required. Fact: Fear intervened to prevent preparation, because of you and your potential. That alone should be empowering! *Can you see it?* Chances are you might lose a few competitions before you identify the weaknesses forced on you. The important point is you now know to look for them. However, once you identify the Type 2 Weakness, you must begin to exercise it to reverse its effect. "How?" Specifically, prepare outside the expected medium and never in the competition arena. It will not be easy, but it is simple. Once you identify the weakness don't make it a factor during the competition. Be careful to remove the Type 2 Weakness from the issue plate as soon as you begin to exercise it. This is an excellent opportunity to exercise common sense. Can you see it unfolding? Also, look for motive where you suspect there is a Forced Weakness working against you. You will soon add it to your strengths column once you master this perspective.

It is easier to focus on strengths than it is to focus on weaknesses. It does not matter on which you focus; both weaknesses and strengths will require your undivided attention at some point. Truth is, both will cost you something in the end. The key is to know them well and to win as often as possible despite them. There are several approaches for you to consider.

The positive thinking and motivating approach says, focus on your strengths and then blow them away with your enthusiasm. I question the exclusive use of strengths even though it often works. The power of positive thinking is awesomely powerful. I practice it daily myself, but from a *get me thru perspective*. My perspective helped me *to see* there is power in knowing as much about my weaknesses as I do about my strengths. Did I hear you ask, "Why and what is the benefit?" I am delighted you asked. It's simple; I am empowered by my strengths, while my enemy is empowered by my weaknesses. *Whew!* It is not necessary for you to become a rocket scientist *to see* this one. If your weaknesses have the ability to empower others, how much more power will you gain by retaining control over them? My point? —What is the one thing champion athletes have in common? Champions always study their opponent's strengths and weaknesses. That diligent practice should not be left on the fields of athletic competition. Remember the Type 1 and 2 weaknesses and keep them out front throughout this exercise. There is wisdom in both.

Here is another good question. "Strengths and weaknesses are a part of everyday living, how then can you exercise your weaknesses and not expose them to others? Actually, the better question is, "How can you exercise weaknesses period?" Now that is a million dollar question. The right answer could well earn you a million dollars, save you a million or cost you a million. The first step in correcting anything is to admit that it does exist. Weaknesses require the same if not more exercise than strengths. The objective for both should always be the same, which is to move forward despite the challenge. The application is also the same. You must put your weaknesses into play as you do your strengths or remove them from the playbook altogether. Athletes employ this strategy all the time and it works. Run the play and as soon as the opponent learns how to read it, change it or stop running it. Am I saying you won't get hit or intercepted? Absolutely not, just not as much! Exercising weaknesses is about toning, increasing muscle, decreasing fat, preserving, strengthening, empowering and more. Weaknesses need practice time, which is why identifying them is so important. The principles of exercise will never change and that is why these spiritual exercises are so powerful! They require you to exercise from the inside out and then some. Remember that weaknesses have the potential to exhaust your strengths. Read the Get Me Thru nugget of wisdom below that inspired this exercise.

"Take more time getting to know your weaknesses and you will spend less time showing them to others."

GMT #1702

This nugget is powerful and it delivers 3 empowering points about Self-Imposed and Forced Weaknesses. Each point will lead you closer *to seeing* how to empower your weaknesses to work for you instead of against you. More importantly, the points will help you *to see* the benefit in exercising your weaknesses. You will also learn how to structure your own program for weaknesses.

Point 1. Everyone Has Weaknesses

Admitting that you have weaknesses is not a cliché, but a true statement. The proof is that man is not perfect. Therefore, weaknesses are destined and it does not take long *to see* them if you are honest. The difficulty however, comes in having to face weaknesses. Unfortunately, for most people denial is a more attractive and seemingly safe alternative. Remember **The Mirror Me Thru Exercise**? I am sure the exercise would have been less challenging had it not required the face-to-face Actions. The humbling fact is that without weaknesses it would be difficult to identify your strengths. *Whew!* That is encouraging, because you are just beyond a weakness the minute you see your strength developing. Likewise, you are just beyond strength the minute you see a weakness. The line is very thin because you are not the only one exercising.

Strengths and weaknesses are joined similarly as survival and getting thru. In other words, the weakness is empowered against you only after you choose to ignore it exist. Conversely, strengths can work for you despite the weaknesses, just not as well.

Remember the cliché, "One man's garbage is another man's treasure"? Guess what? "One man's weakness is another man's strength." I have one more to add, "One man's weakness does not have to empower that man's enemy." Perhaps that is why I am convinced we can exercise weaknesses and by it minimize their exposure to others. I hope you are getting this, because in this sense you are toning and removing the fat.

I actually began the process of identifying my weaknesses as a child. However, I had no idea I was also exercising them then. Children as you know have little fear, except the ones taught to them. I certainly knew as a child I had weaknesses, but it was the strength exercised by other people that brought them light.

Point 2. The Time Factor

Time is a factor that affects everything in life someway or the other. Granted, everyone has the same twenty-four hours in a day, but they are rarely enough. Is there any wonder why so many things go undone? In this case however, the facts clearly dictate the necessary action, which is to take the time. You cannot afford to be passive when it comes to time. You must get aggressive with time. A graduate course on time caused me to focus on it as a major issue. I concluded there are two unchallenged facts about time.

1. Everyone has twenty-four hours in a day.
2. Time will not wait for you to catch up nor will it speed up for you to get ahead.

Essentially, you will have to work harder if you get behind and even harder to get ahead. The fact is, you only have twenty-four hours in a day to get it done. It is just that simple. However, the simplicity of the conclusion does not eliminate the issue. Once again, *the true complexity in life lies in accepting its simplicity.* If you are not careful simplicity will lure you into a zone that is not always productive. In the end, time finds a way to pass you by. It becomes a weakness that takes over your life, but only if you decide not to take control of your time.

The use of time is a huge business, because it is a perceived weakness economically. Think about it for a moment and then read what I just said again. I am not saying time is a vice. Contrary, I am saying that vices rob you of the best use of your time. What then are these vices? They can be anything that takes you away from seeing your goals and dreams through to the end. It does not have to be major. It's funny how we think of chemical dependencies as the worst vices. They are just the more obvious ones. We have countless external and internal vices that cause weaknesses and a loss of focus.

Let me step away for a moment. *I had a problem seeing the benefit in focusing on my weaknesses because my strengths carried me so well. My learning to see weaknesses from a point of empowerment was painfully challenging. Admittedly, I did not want anyone to see my weaknesses . I believed to openly work on weaknesses would have put me at risk of defeat. I must once again credit my MaDear with opening my eyes to nuggets of wisdom. Her wisdom helped me to see the power in working through my own weaknesses.*

The evidence of a particular weakness began to surface during my childhood. We were taught to study hard and learn everything possible to have a better life than our parents. The point was emphasized by one of my MaDear's favorite sayings, "People can't take anything out of your head, so put as much up there as you can." I tried to do just that and as a result, I believed that most of my deposits were right. Consequently, I not only concentrated on gaining knowledge, but also on being right. I had not learned much about wisdom at that point, but I had a lot of knowledge. I did however; learn that when you believe you are right all the time, it leaves little room for growth. My MaDear helped me to see that better than anyone else during a particular situation with my brother.

My brother and I argued often and like most siblings we considered it to be a natural engagement. MaDear's tolerance for our antics lessened after our Daddy's death. She began to emphasize how we should show more love towards each other. Honestly, we thought we were showing love. We certainly didn't treat other people in that way. Actually I did, because arguing for me then was a way of displaying my knowledge. My wisdom wasn't even close to the incubator, but that soon changed.

One day our most drama filled argument lasted way beyond the norm. I remember MaDear passing and looking into the room, but saying nothing. She passed by several times, but never spoke a word. In past times her intervention would not have taken more than a few minutes. We paused a little each time she passed, but resumed as soon as she was out of sight. Her silence was most unusual, but I took it as a confirmation of my being right. Of course, she was just giving me time to really prove my point to my brother.

Then it happened, she finally entered the room. My brother and I stopped arguing immediately and stood staring at her in utter amazement. I spoke first, which you know is the kiss of death if you are selling something. I started out by telling her I was right and that my brother was not listening to me. She listened without interruption as I presented my case. She then allowed my brother the same opportunity, which I did not understand since I was right. My brother and I waited for her to speak. I shall never forget the words she spoke as she carefully placed us directly in front of her. However, she only looked into my eyes, for I had once again made an impatient appeal for her support. Her paralyzing words were:

"DeAtri, I don't know which one of you are right.
But, I do know if I were a stranger passing by,
I would not know which one of you was the fool."

My brother and I just stood in shock and watched her turn and walk out of the room. MaDear's wisdom has been a part of my spiritual resolve since that day. I have repeated her words thousands of times. I learned that day despite my limited capacity, an overwhelming desire to be right often reveals weaknesses to others that you didn't know existed. I had devoted my time exclusively to my strengths and not to my weaknesses. Whew! I am now slow to argue. I am also determined not to reveal unsupported weaknesses before their time.

I broke the first rule of exercising weaknesses. I devoted no time to getting to know my own weaknesses. The result was it caused me to underestimate the strength in others. It also impeded my growth. My MaDear would say *I gagged on gnats and swallowed flies instead*. That is exactly what happens when you fail *to see* your own weaknesses. You give up way too much to get so little in return. Can you *see* that? I did *not see* that weaknesses could still be a problem even if you worked hard on strengths. I relied on one portion of my spirit when I should have focused on the whole. Okay, I hear you saying, but you were just a child. Indeed I was, but I exercised choice and did choose to focus on what I believed to be right. Get it? There's that powerful word *choice* again. The truth is, I lacked the wisdom about balance. I was tipping my own scale. My MaDear did not talk to me about that, but instead she allowed me to experience it. Nevertheless, I learned *to see* the futility in two people talking at once. I had to learn that my weakness was forcing me to assume what was said to me. Haven't you ever wondered why it is that after heated arguments you have trouble remembering the critical points? I also learned to hear what another person is saying by listening first. Unexercised weaknesses are dangerous!

Allow me to step away again for a moment: Weaknesses come into our lives through small and large situations. If you are not careful you will grow old never declaring them. I learned that lesson from an older woman while working at Ford Motor Company in Michigan. I made a very costly assumption while working on a sensitive project. It was fortunate for me that I had endeared myself to her. She caught the mistake just in time and rescued me, but not without asking me a few questions. Her first question was, "Why did you continue…?" My response was, "I assumed that…" She then explained to me on paper, that ASSUME was really an acronym in manufacturing and not just a word. Whew!

My weakness of *being right* and being knowledgeable was still a problem then. Was I setup?–I don't know, but it did not happen again. Her vivid description of the word was pure wisdom and I accepted it. I obviously had to learn more about prioritizing my time, so don't miss the point, in the end it was about time as well.

All in all, my strengths empowered my weaknesses against me, but with my help. Taking the time to know your weaknesses should be a declared act of life, because time itself is universal. It is therefore critical that you define the boundaries under which you use it and protect your granted amount. Inevitably some weaknesses will show, but you can still reveal and exercise them on your terms.

Point 3. You Pay a Price When People See Your Weaknesses…

Everything cost something, whether it is money or time. Both have measurable and immeasurable values. The key in this instance is discerning which is the most valuable to you at an appointed time. I assure you the price rises and falls depending on who discovers the weakness first. It's ironic, but the one who discovers the weakness first tends to keep it to himself, but why? The answer is commanding if you are the discoverer. You keep it until you need to use it. You bet my brother knew which one of my buttons to push to get me out of sink. Foolishly, I thought I was at my best in arguing with him, when I was no doubt at my worst. I paid for it every time he lured me into his brilliant web. Each time I argued I abandoned an opportunity to be fed by wisdom. I risked concentration, patience and the opportunity *to hear* what was being said to me. Arguing misrepresents your ability to listen and then forces you to respond prematurely, because the adrenaline is so rampant. Hearing requires a communion with your spirit and that revelation only comes through wisdom. Don't miss this point. I can't tell how many hind sighted days I experienced after an argument. It was because of my unsupported weakness to be right and it cost me.

I hope you have a glimpse of how unassuming and dangerous our weaknesses can become. They can fly right under the radar for your entire life. That one weakness discovered during my childhood redirected my personality, goals and a lot more. One lifetime carrot is, I continue to focus on *hearing* what people say to me, which requires time and meditative thinking.

Let me share one other point about time before I put you to work. Extremely successful people seem to pop up out of nowhere. In other words, it's like they were always there. Only a few people remember when Bill Gates and Oprah Winfrey weren't successful and wealthy. I assure you their success causes competitors to focus on their strengths and most especially their weaknesses. Do you think for one minute that Ms. Winfrey and Mr. Gates don't devote prioritized efforts to minimizing their weaknesses? I am not a gambler, but I am willing to wager you that they are in touch with their weaknesses. Therefore, they are rarely caught by surprise when others attempt to use their weaknesses against them. Granted, the price of exposing their weaknesses is relative, but nonetheless costly. Also, the price is certain to include time and recovery is always costly. Do you see it?

"Weaknesses exercised outside your spiritual boundaries makes it easy for others to disrupt your spirituality."

I am convinced you are in possession of an internal incubator that stores volumes of wisdom meant just for you. However, the incubator requires that you regard the foundation upon which your intended wisdom is based. In other words, you must go back and pick up the wisdom. Do not confuse this with going backwards, because you are not. You are simply preparing to move forward.

"Wisdom like time is universal,
except you can go back to it."

However, it too will not wait for you nor will it speed up to get you ahead. Wisdom is there for everyone to experience. You must seek it and be prepared for it once you learn *to see it.* I have clarified this point throughout this chapter.

Let's talk about going back. There is something magical about reflecting into your childhood days and that includes the unhappy days as well. Here is a word of caution. I am not talking about the psychological approach to uncovering deep dark secrets. I am referring to spiritual empowerment and uncovering a foundation for wisdom that you somehow may have missed. I believe it is nearly impossible to commune with human beings and not be exposed to some wisdom. One would have to commit to daily practices of ignorance to avoid some wisdom. I know that sounds harsh, but Coaches need to be harsh at times. Such deep reflection compels a level of thinking that only you and your spirit will understand. Perhaps that is why I believe few people will know the impact of being in that room with my MaDear and brother. Only God and I know for sure. You too have a few of those wisdom filled episodes in your life, so let's uncover a few of them. Don't worry, I am going to help you. What you need is already within you and my mission is to help you *to see* it. Now, let's address the objective of this exercise and your going back to a few memorable episodes.

The objective of this exercise is to help you identify some weaknesses and to find supportive wisdom to exercise them. Your success is contingent on your spiritual perspective during this exercise. I therefore need you to view this exercise as a Get Me Thru Workshop using my definition. My definition of this type of workshop is: *A relationship in which, I as your Coach do the work while you shop through my words and perspectives until you find inspiration. Once you identify a point of inspiration you must commit to go to work.* My goal for this entire book is that you find inspiration and not necessarily motivation. I could never write enough to keep you motivated. However, one nugget of spiritual inspiration that leads to wisdom could last you a lifetime.

Whew!

Everyone's past includes Memorable Episodes. *A memorable episode is any situation from which you learned a lesson that remains in your spirit.* It does not matter that you do not currently practice the lesson. Each of my childhood examples represented a memorable episode. Thankfully, I have lessons of wisdom from them that yet enrich my life. Perform the following actions in your Peaceful Location. You will need solitude for several minutes to successfully complete the exercises. You will not experience success if you are interrupted.

ACTION: Reflect on your past until you uncover at least 2-3 memorable episodes. The episode could even be a consistent word of wisdom taught to you that you never forgot.
ACTION: Write down one point of weakness for each episode and one point of wisdom. Remember, memorable episodes will never leave you empty-handed, so dig for clarification.

Memorable Episode #1:

Point of Weakness:

Point of Wisdom:

Memorable Episode #2:

Point of Weakness:

Point of Wisdom:

Memorable Episode #3:

Point of Weakness:

Point of Wisdom:

ACTION: Rewrite and classify the weaknesses you identified in your three Memorable Episodes:

Self-Imposed-Type 1 or Forced-Type 2

Type 1___ Type 2 ___ ☐ ☐ Weakness #1.

____

____

____

____

Type 1___ Type 2 ___ ☐ ☐ Weakness #2.

____

____

____

____

Type 1___ Type 2 ___ ☐ ☐ Weakness #3.

____

____

____

____

ACTION: Place a check in the box by each weakness you are willing to exercise.

ACTION: Place a second check in the box by each weakness for which you gained a nugget of wisdom. You may also consider nuggets of wisdom from this book.

ACTION: Write down one nugget of wisdom about a weakness you will honor and exercise.

____

____

____

ACTION: Read the following statement and sign your name only if you agree.

I, ______________________________commit to exercising my weaknesses using nuggets of wisdom as my inspiration and guide.

Date:____________________

ACTION: Read the Life-Style challenge and then meditate on it for a few minutes. Afterwards, you are to respond to the charges made against you.

Life-Style Challenge: The laws have been changed and everyone has been declared Guilty Until Proven Innocent. The charges and lifetime imprisonment are the same for everyone. However, you have the opportunity to defend yourself against all charges.

- Guilty of Physical Neglect
- Guilty of Being a Quitter
- Guilty of Dishonesty
- Guilty of Unhealthy Life-Style
- Guilty of Lying to Self
- Guilty of Hypocrisy
- Guilty of Self-Pity
- Guilty of Procrastination
- Guilty of Not Taking Time For Self

Regarding your imprisonment, the new law has also declared that release is contingent on your meeting certain requirements. You must present an acceptable plan of action proving your innocence. You alone must present and prepare your defense. Everyone is given thirty days to prepare and present his or her defense. The law further requires you to address your use of time and all identified weaknesses, as they are considered accomplices in your charges. Consider the following questions as you prepare your defense.

- Are you confident enough today to stand before a judge?
- Have you identified weaknesses and strengths to support your defense?

- Are there charges you can eliminate now? If so, can you use the defense to support other charges? Look carefully.
- What would you do differently today if this were a real life scenario?

Remember this Get Me Thru nugget: "No Comparing, No Complaining, but Setting a Standard." You are reckoning with your weaknesses, taking back control of your time, and setting a new standard of care and respect for you.

Let me leave you with a few examples of weaknesses that can fly under the radar for your defense. If unattended, such weaknesses can leave you vulnerable. Remember the unassuming ones can be dangerous. Here they are:

- So busy doing good that you are convinced it is okay to neglect yourself.
- Lack of discernment regarding, "What is love?" and "Who is a friend?"
- No daily practices toward your goals and dreams
- Fill entire days without setting aside personal time
- Always respond 'Yes' to avoid saying why 'No' is better for you
- Stand on the side of pride much too long
- Saying, "I was wrong" is painful
- Saying, "I don't know" is painful
- Refuse to believe the mirror doesn't lie

ACTION: Develop your Plan of Action and Defense. Check the charges you accept and write down your Plan of Action for release. You must also write a Defense for the charges you do not accept.

Guilty of Physical Neglect: Accept_____ Do Not Accept_____
Defense:

Plan of Action:

Guilty of Lying to Self: Accept_____ Do Not Accept_____
Defense:

Plan of Action:

Guilty of Being a Quitter: Accept_____ Do Not Accept_____
Defense:

Plan of Action:

____

____

____

____

____

Guilty of Hypocrisy: Accept_____ Do Not Accept_____

Defense:

____

____

____

____

____

Plan of Action:

____

____

____

____

____

Guilty of Not Taking Time for Self:
Accept_____ Do Not Accept_____

Defense:

____

____

____

____

____

Plan of Action:

____

Guilty of Dishonesty: Accept_____ Do Not Accept_____

Defense:

Plan of Action:

Guilty of Unhealthy Life-style:
Accept_____ Do Not Accept_____

Defense:

Plan of Action:

____

____

____

____

____

Guilty of Procrastination: Accept_____ Do Not Accept_____
Defense:

____

____

____

____

____

Plan of Action:

____

____

____

____

____

Guilty of Self-Pity/Low-Self Esteem:
Accept_____ Do Not Accept_____

Defense and Plan of Action:

____

____

____

____

____

____

____

Weaknesses are opportunities to get stronger. They are also stepping stones, but they will trip you if you don't learn exactly where to step! Did you get that?

"Exercise your weaknesses by identifying them, classifying them and then by putting them into action on your terms."

Afterwards, weigh your spiritual resolve daily against their strength and watch your muscle grow. Where you step after that becomes clearer.

Remember, the law granted you thirty days to prepare your defense. You may therefore come back to this exercise should you need to do so. Completing the remaining exercises before addressing your defense may strengthen it, but I will let you be the judge.

However, check *to see* if anything in your responses will change the results in your **Becoming You Model**. If so, go back and make the necessary adjustments. I trust you are beginning *to see* more through each exercise. If not, you are not working hard enough.

Lastly, you and I know that this scenario is unlikely to happen. However, which would be worst for you: *Physical imprisonment or spiritual imprisonment?* This exercise can help to release you from one of them for sure! Remember this nugget of wisdom.

"It requires more energy to hide your weaknesses during war than it does to convert them to strengths during peace time."

ACTION: As always, take a few deep breaths and be sure to secure your book and pencil after you finish. See you later for your next exercise.

A Get Me Thru Nugget Of Wisdom:

"Not exercising weaknesses is like running around your backhand in tennis. It wears you out, but not before exposing your weakness to your opponent and everyone else watching."

CHAPTER EIGHT

CHALLENGING CHANGE

Change is not an easy issue to exercise. It is challenging and sometimes painful. Change is also empowering when you are guided by *the voice of your boundaries.* On the other hand, changes made independent of the voice of your boundaries are tricks against your spirit and are destined to fail. In fact, changes in your life that are not life-style changes will cause you to lie to yourself over and over and again. If that is not a trick against your spirit I don't know what is, and guess what? If you lie to yourself, that makes you a liar, even if you are the only other one who knows about it. I decided to press hard from the beginning with this chapter, so you may need to take a few breaks before you finish. Reality sometimes hurts and I am not searching here. I am writing from experiences that developed into nuggets of wisdom. I gladly admit this chapter was inspired long ago by a special Get Me Thru nugget of wisdom. It constantly inspires my spirit and I pray its depth inspires you as well.

"Remember: When you decide to make changes that affect your life, you must also be prepared to make **those changes for the rest of your life."**

GMT #1716

This nugget about commitment is powerful and full of inspiration. Can you see it? The caution *to remember* lets you know that with change, it is easier to retreat, so watch out. The second point is that change does affect your whole life and not just a circumstance. Third, change requires preparation and it must be for the rest of your life. All else is a temporary fix. Remember it is easy to believe otherwise when you live outside your spiritual boundaries. Consider these questions about change for me please. There is no assessment for them. I just want you to consider them as you continue, because questions are powerful revelations. You can always refuse to accept answers, but questions stay with you. *Whew!*

- When was the last time you made a change in your life?
- Did the change have any lasting affects on your life?
- Was there anything about the change that requires your daily attention?
- Did you prepare for the change?
- If no, would preparation have helped?
- Did you commit to exercise the change for the rest of your life?
- Did the *voice of your boundaries* dictate the change?
- Are you still practicing the change?

Change requires commitment and that alone is intimidating. The need for commitment should have been seen in the questions you just considered. Have you ever wondered why it is that so many men are afraid of commitment? Admittedly, their fear does make sense to me. I must also confess that such resolve is from spiritual wisdom. My conclusion is God gave men an innate view of the synonymous relationship between commitment and change. The fact is, you cannot separate the two. Commitment means something has to change and that can be scary. Why?—Because most people are content in their reluctance to change, and to act contrary to it is uncomfortable. The Get Me Thru perspective on commitment and change is for the whole of life.

"Enduring change enriches your spirituality, while temporary fixes present an illusion of it."

Dieting is an excellent example of a temporary fix, and I can prove my point with a simple question. "Is the need for dieting more often the result of a practiced life-style or something else?" The honest answer is, *the need for dieting is most often the result of a practiced life-style.* Why then do intelligent people approach it with temporary fixes? The answer is that it's easier. No doubt, change is difficult, but to conquer it you must address it from a *whole of life* perspective.

Actually, if you address change from an economic perspective, temporary fixes are more profitable. Why?—Again the answer is simple, because temporary fixes assure the market of your repeat business. Those who study your behavior have already determined the average individual is lazy. I said it and you have my permission to shoot the messenger if the message is not true. I dare researchers to trace the causes of wars and tragedies and not find that a quick fix or the resistance to change weakened the links. Temporary fixes are like survival, as they are designed to get you started, but not to get you thru. Here are 4 tips about temporary fixes that I want you to consider.

1. Temporary fixes are like part-time jobs that pay you, but they do not offer long-term benefits.
2. Temporary fixes are deceptive, because they take your focus away from the importance of permanency.
3. Temporary fixes are calculated by others and tailored to your compromised life-style to control your growth.

4. Temporary fixes discourage long-term exercise, because of the instant gratification.

Likewise, let me give you 10 tips about change:

1. Change is a permitted test of faith afforded your enemy, while God weighs your spirit. A test of faith should never be considered without also considering weighing your spirit. I am convinced that change is an inevitable mystery designed by God to *weigh your spirit* and not to necessarily test it. This perspective may seem odd, so let me explain. I use the word mystery to say the completeness of it all is not available to man's understanding. Therefore, humankind is only privileged to the essence of change. Needlessly to say, everyone is affected by it in someway. So, what do I mean by, *to weigh your spirit and not to test it*? Excellent question. I believe faith supremely gives weight to your spirit. Faith keeps you grounded. Faith fuels your endurance, because it causes you to act on the unseen for that which you have seen only through your spirit. Do you see it now? Consider the biblical story about Job. God obviously gave the devil an open hand *to change* everything in Job's life. One second all his children were in fellowship and rejoicing together and the next second they all lay dead, — *a change.* One second he owned thousands of cattle and livestock and the next second they were either stolen or killed, —*a change*. One second Job was healthy and happy and the next second he suffered in the foul of his sores praying that death had come before his conception,— *a change*. God knew the devil perceived it to be a test only and not a plan to bless Job. Now, I know Solomon shares that God does tests the hearts. God also allows the enemy of your spiritual resolve to test your faith. I believe that tests of the spirit are against your enemy and for your empowerment. *Whew!* To believe otherwise would mean you were setup by God, which is absurd. Tests present you opportunities to increase your spiritual weight and that is the one thing your enemy will never understand. Even Solomon agrees with this point!

Remember a test is designed to expose what you know. However, faith allows you to move forward despite the test because of added faithfulness. Had it been just a test by God Job would have failed. Job clearly did not know enough to pass the test, but he gained it during the test. Besides, man is still analyzing Job's triumph. Consider this, a Sunday School class member of mine shared that her father often shouted to the preacher, "Put your weight on it." I could not agree more when it comes to tests and spiritual resolve. What a delightful way to describe the power in the weight of your faith and spirituality.

In the end, Job's faith in God gave sufficient weight to his spirit. God then blessed him once again beyond measure. Do we understand it all? No, but I certainly do not believe God will set you up for failure. Contrary, I believe He sets the stage through change to increase faith and grant wisdom. It is rare that lifetime change does not yield wisdom and an increased faith.

Allow me to further expound on Job's problem. He was forced to show his hand to God and to the devil, because death was not an alternative. The devil, being a foe and not a friend sought to attack the physical while God's purpose for Job was to allow him *to see* the power of the spirit that dwelled within him. Again, if this were God's test, Job would have failed! This was a test that God allowed the devil to process. Read a few of the discourses in the Bible for yourself and I am certain you will agree. Job's perseverance was borne out of his added weight through his renewed faith in God. There was a point in the story where Job actually began to lose weight, but he quickly recovered as he began to listen to the voice of his boundaries. Job's foundation was in his faith in God and that gave weight to his spirit. Job is perhaps one of the more difficult stories to comprehend, but it is all about perspective. HINT: The weight of your spirit determines the firmness of your spiritual foundation. If we were actually tested by God, we would fail and die much to soon. *Do you see it?* This is an empowering perspective, so I hope you see it. Pause here for a moment and ponder these points. There is wisdom here and where you find wisdom; you will also find a blessing. Don't forget, *the true complexity in life is accepting its simplicity.* Perhaps that is why resistance to change is so strong and the failure rate is so high. It does not have to be that way and a different perspective just maybe the answer. Here are nine more perspectives about change.

2. Change is a necessary course of life *to see* wisdom.
3. Change enables the inner spirit to redirect pathways during challenges.
4. Change provokes thinking and leads to invaluable questions.
5. Change is universal and no one is immune.
6. Change is inspired because of questions and not necessarily by answers.
7. Change indents the footprints of life.
8. Change is introduced by external motivation, initiated by encouragement and seen through to the end by inspiration and wisdom.
9. Change typically follows FEAR and FEAR typically leads to temporary fixes except when lead by the voice of your boundaries.
10. Change weighs your spirit, because to test it may require your life. However, death in such spiritual exercises is not God's purpose.

Effective change must align with your spiritual boundaries or you are subjecting yourself to a test you will fail. Everyone will be compelled to change something in life, but few will commit to specific changes for the rest of their lives. Don't miss this nugget. Perhaps, that is why we have more of the economically *have-nots* than we do *the haves*. The haves practice what the have-nots are unwilling to practice. The haves also teach generations that follow to do the same. Pause with me for a moment and consider these questions that add clarity to the spirituality of change and temporary fixes. "What are fads? Are fads not temporary by design? Are they not money-makers? Who actually benefits from the temporary fixes that fads offer? Can you use fads to your advantage?" Don't miss the point, because this is not an indictment against making money. I am just helping you *to see* a perspective regarding the important nature of real change. Admittedly, fads are here to stay and neither you nor I will ever change that fact. Nevertheless, do you see how costly temporary fixes can be without the right perspective about change? The answers fit into one neat response, "Fads are temporary market reactions that separate consumers from their money while also responding to requests for quick fixes." Fads have a foundation that is stabilized by economic cycles and greed. The question is, where do you fit in such a scheme? I will tell you the answer is in your perspective and foundation.

Interestingly, most people say they accept that change is certain and valuable. The problem comes in timing and implementation. A friend of mine owned a beautiful convertible Mercedes Benz. She proudly displayed a very bold message on her rear bumper that read, "S_ _ _ Happens!" I asked her why did she put that somewhat profane statement on her car. She responded without hesitation, "Venita, S_ _ _ does happen!" I conceded and thought, case closed. However, it did not go away easily for me. I pondered her statement for several years as I watched more of life unfold around me. I concluded that Yes, "S_ _ _ does happen", but as a form of change. My friend's bumper sticker was a true, but crude description of it. All in all, we do expect things to happen, but it is eventually the timing of it that rocks our world. It also forces us to exercise temporary fixes rather than the required life-style changes.

I introduced you to 3 critical points earlier. Let's review them, as you will need them in this chapter as well.

1. You must initiate and maintain changes for the rest of your life.

2. Your spiritual foundation controls your growth, victories and defeats.

3. Neglected weaknesses will empower your enemies.

I have learned that one of the many reactions to change is stress. Most people will tell you stress fuels them to victory. It causes them to call on resources they otherwise would never use. The interesting thing about those declarations is most of them are true, yet potentially deadly. Stress can fly under the radar for a very longtime and misrepresent necessary changes using that perspective. Stress is dangerous and often indicative of a resistance to change. I know, because my ignorance of the relationship between the resistance to change and stress nearly cost me my life. I hope you will see how easily the need for change can fly under the radar of your spiritual resolve.

On that note, let me step away for a few minutes and introduce you to The Pressure Cooker Effect. This is my favorite Wisdom Episode. I am convinced it is a Wisdom Episode that will touch your life in a meaningful way as well, so here it is:

Pressure is a word most adults accept as a part of daily living. A more acceptable term is called stress. Whether your stress is pressure or whether your pressure is stress, the effect on your life is most likely the same. I trust at this point you are nodding in affirmation. Of course, I did not process the relationship as well as a child even though I was constantly exposed to it. It was years into my adulthood before the light began to clarify wisdom and even then not before I mastered pausing.

While growing up in the small mining town of Docena, I witnessed many scrumptious meals courtesy of my MaDear. Our Sunday dinners were adjusted versions of Christmas and Thanksgiving dinners. We enjoyed ham hocks, neck bones, black-eyed peas, collard greens and corn bread, fried chicken and more. The collard greens, which by the way are still my favorite vegetable, were labor-intensive. My daddy, while a coal miner was also a farmer. He had to plant the seedlings, work the garden, harvest the greens and my MaDear picked and cleaned them. While picking them was quite a chore, washing and cutting them was an art form. The ham hocks and the seasonings represented the backbone for most good cooks of collard greens. The pot-liquor from the ham hocks did the trick and a tenderized ham hock also required much time. All this preparation and the greens were yet to be cooked. I smile now even thinking about how the smell drove me to unjustified hunger pains. Oh, the power of aromas!

Well, I always believed my MaDear was ahead of her time. Although, equipped with only a sixth grade education, she was blessed with a brilliance that yet amazes me. She saved a little money from this and a little from that and purchased a Pressure Cooker. I did not know that my elementary knowledge of her Pressure Cooker would play a vital role in my life and now in yours as well. I watched my MaDear cook countless meals in her Pressure Cooker for many years.

She learned more about it with each use and it became more than just a pot to her. I could tell by the way she pampered her high priced jewel. It represented freedom and allowed her to enjoy cooking all the more. My MaDear learned that her pot was designed to operate at its best under tremendous pressure. More importantly, she learned to respect the pressure the pot held. Remember the point earlier about how some people do their best work under pressure? That's a good point to remember throughout this chapter.

What does this episode have to do with change? The answer is more than you thought you knew. It took my MaDear several meals before she learned the pressure harnessed in the pot was her friend and not a foe. That is, it was her friend as long as she released the pressure properly, which she did every time. I read product instructions today because of that pressure cooker. The instructions stated clearly that to improperly release the pressure could destroy the pot and cause physical harm. Don't miss this point! In essence, storing stress or pressure is not a bad thing. The harm comes in not releasing it and in how it is released. The revelation meant change for me or to exercise the alternative and end up like a misused Pressure Cooker. I also learned I was a living pressure cooker and that I could learn a lot about releasing pressure from the care guide of a steel pot. The instructions for the pot gave MaDear two choices for releasing the pressure:

1. *Release the pressure after allowing the pot to cool down completely.*
2. *Release the pressure by running cold-water over-the-top until all the pressure dissipated.*

The key was accepting that releasing pressure was a process that should be followed every time there was a build up of pressure. Did that require my MaDear to implement a change during her cooking? You bet it did. First, there were only certain things she could cook in that particular pot and second, she had to monitor the pressure build up and release it accordingly. She did not have the luxury of choice in the matter if she desired to preserve the pot for long-term use, which she did. Pressure or stress is the same whether the vessel is steel or flesh! Are you seeing the point yet? Stay with me and I am going to make it clear.

"The right perspective inspires wisdom and courage!"

Several years ago I was forced to regard personal stress the same as my MaDear had regarded her Pressure Cooker or give up life as

I knew it. The latter was not my choice. Therefore, I had to implement some changes for the rest of my life. Whew!

A somehow compromised surgery forced me to get to know my body, which required a multitude of changes. This Get Me Thru nugget of wisdom helped me to see the merit in a new perspective on lifetime changes, though the difficulty remained.

"Get to know your body now or the day is sure to come when you won't recognize it, and it will refuse to acknowledge you."
GMT #1715

The surgery forced me to live without a few body parts. I first became acquainted with the functions of my forfeited organs and learned how to compensate for their absence. I changed my life-style accordingly. I implemented a supplemental nutritional program and exercised regularly. I was very active so the latter was not difficult. I did not however change the way I processed stress very well. I stored it and kept on going. Remember wisdom is often forced, while still requiring payment.

My abbreviated changes carried me for a few years more and then near disaster hit again. I was diagnosed with a runaway thyroid. That is my term, because that is how it made me feel. My heartbeats were way ahead of me and my breath gave out way to soon. My weight was uncontrollable and I assure you I did not have any to lose. I crawled up my stairs for fear of falling. There were few answers, until after much pleading, my doctor agreed that it wasn't just in my head. Tests revealed that my thyroid was hyperactive. It wasn't just hyperactive; it was nearly off the scale. I was often awake for days at a time. I was in great danger. I was relieved just to know the culprit. However, I found myself once again faced with the need for changes.

Truthfully, I had no knowledge of the thyroid except I knew that I had no intention of parting with it. I made that vow to God and to me. I promised God after I survived my last surgery that I would meet Him with all my remaining organs. I therefore asked my respected endocrinologist what caused my thyroid to overproduce and what were the prescribed treatments. She informed me that no one really knew the cause, but my options were twofold. My choices were removal of the thyroid and lifetime medication or nuclear iodine therapy and lifetime medication. RED LIGHT! I was not as disturbed by the treatment options as I was by the fact that no one knew the cause. Surely, you know the next question, "How do you know the iodine or surgery is the best treatment for me?" Her response, "Venita, we have done it this way for the past 50 years and our patients do exceptionally well." Please understand that I am thankful for the treatments available for they have saved the lives of hundreds of thousands. However, my fear and vow caused me to seek alternative courses. I believed I had a better chance of keeping my thyroid if I knew the cause and my questions were to that specific end. I also realized I needed time. I asked her how long could I remain on the prescribed PTU capsules to regulate my thyroid. I took them around the clock. Her response of six months to a year gave me the time I needed. I told her that removal was not a considered alternative. I left her office, which was approximately two hours from my home, determined to find a way to keep my thyroid and vow. I made a common sense decision not to shoot in the dark, but to seek the cause.

"Change is a life-style commitment and not a temporary fix."

I researched volumes for information about the thyroid and I was surprised to learn the power of my precious little butterfly image. I learned it was the processing unit for my metabolic functions. When my thyroid was out of harmony, so was everything else. Most of my research was depressing, which was the last thing I needed. Whew! I was desperate to find someone who knew the cause of my problem. It took a while, but I did find a wonderful doctor in Florida who was well acquainted with thyroid diseases. My first question was, "What causes the thyroid to overproduce thyroxin?" He answered me by sharing that thyroid disease was one of the first diseases linked to stress. Needlessly to say, I was floored by his response. Aha, my MaDear's Pressure Cooker was paying off in more ways than one. Now all I needed to know was how to process the kind of pressure or stress he was describing. Once again, it was all about change. I had to learn that stress was more than panic attacks, anxiety or strokes. Stress was actually a quiet element that flies under the spiritual radar until it implodes. It is like the Pressure Cooker, except the pressure build up in our bodies. However, we carelessly forget it is there and that creates a problem. I rarely released my pressure, but added to it daily without fail. My body had been forgiving and responsive until it had no more to give. When I failed to release the stress, I allowed it to setup house and left it no alternative but to turn on me. Turn on me is an understatement. I was at the point of implosion! I did some of my best work under pressure, but with reckless disregard to my body and that was dumb.

I suspect the one who designed the Pressure Cooker Pot used our bodies as a model. It was a brilliant idea that undoubtedly will withstand the test of time. Pressure is actually a wonderful incentive for progress when properly applied and processed. Releasing the pressure is the key, so how did I make the concept work for my situation? I remembered MaDear had a steel weight for her pot to help her regulate the pressure for various foods. It was an applicable parallel, which meant that I too had to find a way to weigh my stress.

My new doctor proposed an alternative approach to restoring my health, but I wasn't prepared for such change. Therefore, I continued to take my PTUs because it was the most acceptable choice of the three for me at that time. However, I also read materials provided by my Florida doctor. I discovered that his approach to good health gave more credence to the Pressure Cooker Effect than

I had previously discovered. I shared with my new doctor that I had believed my approach to stress to be successful before reading his material. I proudly proclaimed to him how I had survived tragedies in my life. I knew few people had seen me sweat and surely that meant that I conquered my stress—wrong! After patiently listening to me, he asked the question that helped to change my life and I pray you see it. He asked, "Venita, how are you releasing your daily stress?" "Uh-Uh-what do you mean?", I asked. That my dear reader is a nonintellectual response for, "Not at all." Remember the fundamentals of the Pressure Cooker Pot? Pause here for a few minutes...

Opening such a pot even today, before properly releasing the pressure is a prescription for disaster and replacement parts, and I had no desire for either. Of course, our bodies tend not to have such an immediate reaction to stored stress, which makes the eventual effect all the more frightening. I learned that releasing my stress daily was just as important as it was for my MaDear to release the pressure from her pot after each use. Here it comes! I had to impose some changes, but not temporarily. My changes had to be for the whole of life and for the rest of my life. Whole means I had to focus on my whole body and not merely the symptoms I presented to the good doctor. Whew! I had to resort to deep soul-searching about where I stood.

My Florida doctor helped when he proposed something that put my resolve to the crowning test. He asked me to document as much as possible about my diseases and illnesses, covering both my childhood and adulthood. I asked him exactly what did he mean. He made it plain by stating, anything I considered to be stressful during or near a time of illness and to specify the illness. I thought that was simple enough since I only needed to cover forty plus years. Certainly, he wasn't serious, but he was indeed serious. Can you imagine the challenge? I pray that you can! Out of fear, I did not carry out his request immediately. However, the unknown soon got the best of me and I jumped in with determination. The more I wrote the more stress I was able to identify. The apparent link between the stress and my health incidences were quite interesting. Can you believe this concession, coming from a person who grew up with a pressure-cooking MaDear?

After informing me in ambiguous medical terms, my good doctor began to speak a language that I understood–questions. My answers were predictable; poor eating habits, good exercise habits and absolutely no planned stress release program. In the end, my score card did not look good. Thank God for grace and mercy…

I remember saying to him that discovering my culprit could not be as simple as that. His reply was, it was a very simple approach. Aha – the complexity in life once again is in accepting its simplicity. Admittedly, he never once implied that it was easy. He reminded me that most people end up having their thyroid removed and that was all I needed to hear. My new prescription was threefold: 1. Skilled Daily Meditation, 2. Whole Foods and 3. Exercise. The most challenging was to eliminate processed foods, which included white sugar. Oh, What a change! By the way, I did not sever my relationship with my two other doctors. They were keeping me regulated with the PTU as I explored my alternative care programs. I did not decide to follow my new doctor's program for quite a while. He convinced me it would require a life-style change and I understood what he meant. I therefore, did not approach it lightly. I decided to spend quality time with myself and reflect. I searched my life for inspiration to see such a change through. You guessed it- I went back to my MaDear's Pressure Cooker for inspiration. The principle was the same, even though the application had to be adjusted. I didn't go on a diet, because that was a temporary fix. I did not join a health club, because I knew I would not remain loyal to the regime. I also did not go through the motions of Yoga and claim to be a guru. My approach was to first study all three alternatives and then determine the best strategy for each. I bought books for all three and pressed hard until I could see myself in them. It eventually happened, and I began to change my life-style and little by little over the course of nearly a year, my PTU prescription was reduced to zero. Did you ask, "Was it difficult to make and maintain the changes?" My answer is "Yes, and that it is still a challenge." However, it is a challenge I am willing to live for…

I just shared another Wisdom Episode. I am convinced everyone is blessed with them. However, it is difficult *to see* them. They are most often revealed to you upon searching your spirit. My task now is to convince you that you too have life-changing support in your own Wisdom Episodes. However, you must do the work to uncover them. My episodes are to help you *to see* how wisdom can be found in otherwise uncommon situations. This again is one of the many mysteries of God. You attempted to uncover some in the previous exercise. However, let's try another approach now that you have experienced another one of my episodes. This exercise may take a few days, so don't get impatient.

ACTION: You are to spend quiet time in your Peaceful Location reflecting from your childhood to where you are today. Make notes about one specific experience involving a change that yet occupies space in your spirit. This experience should cause you to think and rethink decisions even today. Chances are, you still resist its wisdom only to battle with your conscience. Consider the following questions while describing the experience.

1. Where did the experience take place?
2. How old were you when it occurred?
3. Did the experience occur near a health episode?
4. Explain the wisdom you gained from the experience.

ACTION: Summarize your experience into a nugget of wisdom.

ACTION: Write down 1 nugget of wisdom from this book that inspires you to exercise life-altering changes.

YOU MUST FIND INSPIRATION TO CHANGE! Oh, I am shouting again, but remember I don't know you and sometimes I shout to keep you alert. I want your attention here, so please don't settle for less from this exercise. It may well give you back life. Remember that wisdom for change comes from the unlikeliest sources and you will never master change without wisdom.

A Get Me Thru Nugget Of Wisdom:

"Change is introduced by inspiration,
exercised by choice and
carried out through new practices."

CHAPTER NINE

A GET ME THRU PARTNERSHIP

Welcome back from Challenging Change! I hope you didn't stop before receiving your own nugget of wisdom. I assure you any difficulty you experienced was worth it.

This chapter may be your easiest or most difficult, as you are about to select a Get Me Thru Partner. This partner represents a needed support base for the remainder of this program. You will appreciate having a partner, because spiritual exercising will benefit you and those in your life. Specifically, it benefits the individual who is the closest in spirit and in trust to you. It is difficult for you *to see* all sides of anything. Perhaps that is why the saying that *no one is an island* is accepted universally. That statement could not be truer than when it comes to moving beyond surviving and onto getting thru, which has been the goal of each exercise so far.

Getting thru requires you to face challenges head on. You must then exercise the challenges of change for the rest of your life as you just learned. Accepting anything for the rest of your life is frightening and I know that places you at a crossroad. Therefore, you can stay where you are in this program or you can decide to move forward. However you cannot move forward alone. You must choose a Get Me Thru Partner to continue. Why?—Because getting thru requires changes, challenges, wisdom, strength, commitment, laughter, tears, sweat and old fashioned guts. It is not a healthy practice to face them alone. I must confess, the depth of the Get Me Thru nugget of wisdom that inspired this chapter was withheld from me until I began to write the final draft of this book. It took me more than five years to understand its place in my story, but here it is:

"A stranger stopped me one day and quickly removed a knife from my back. I hesitated to accept it had really been removed from my flesh. It was then the stranger pointed out that He had removed many before and felt I needed to know."
GMT #3719

This particular Get Me Thru nugget was placed in my spirit late one night several years ago. I was talking on the telephone with a cousin and felt an urge to write. I asked if I could call her back. I wrote it on my bedside pad and quickly called her back. I told her I had just been given a puzzling nugget of wisdom and read it to her. We both were taken aback by the implication. She asked, "Where did that come from?" My response was, "From God, but I don't know why He gave it to me." I actually avoided discussing it with anyone because I did not have a personal point of reference for its meaning. I did have a point of reference for all the others and never had to force a meaning for any of them. I had no plan of doing so with this one.

Ideally, I could say that *no one is an island* and *everyone needs someone,* or even parallel it to the *footprints in the sand*. However, I was never lead to say any of those things about that nugget. It found its own space and who knew it would be through an exercise for this kind of support.

Remember, the true complexity in life is accepting its simplicity. Well, here it is! The stranger isn't a stranger at all, but is the Spirit residing within you. The Spirit manifests itself in many ways to make sure you acknowledge the existence of an omnipotent power. The blessings are unavoidably obvious. How many times have you actually wondered, "How did I get through that one?" Actually, it was your faith and *the stranger*. This exercise presents the stranger as always being there, but it also presses the need for a physical support base to help you in acknowledging the stranger. Why?—Because it is good to have another person who sees what you *see* as well. These exercises represent the beginning of things to come for your life. You will begin to take on a renewed strength with an adjusted perspective about life. You are going to need the hand of:

- Someone whose personal and spiritual mirror is also a true reflection of them
- Someone who understands how deeply An Exercise of Spiritual Boundaries can affect a person's life
- Someone who has seen himself through the Becoming You Model
- Someone who takes time getting to know their own weaknesses
- Someone who is strong enough to Challenge Change. That someone is a Get Me Thru Partner. It should not be difficult, because you already answered several relevant questions in Chapter Six. Let's review those that are applicable to this exercise. I am listing the questions by their actual numbers from the chapter. You may need to refer to your answers before making your final decision about your partner. On the other hand, you may want to change some answers now that you have a few exercises under your belt.

7. Will the person closest to you say you hear better or that you listen better?
Who is that person?

---

8. Is there anyone in your life who would see the same person who came through during **The Mirror Me Thru Exercise**? **Who is that person?**

---

11. Do you speak openly about your inner spirit to anyone?
Who is that person?

---

76. Would your best friend say they are pleased with the way you are treating their best friend—who is you?
Who is that person?

---

78. Who is the person whom you trust the most and why?

---

80. Regarding question #78, would your responses to any of the questions in this book surprise that person?
Who is that person again?

---

87. Who is the person with whom you would share all of your answers from this book?

ACTION: Use these questions to help in your selection or you may add others. Please know that this should not be a rushed decision. I encourage you to give this exercise sincere thought. On that note, I have three more questions that may help you.

- Who is the one person with whom you can share intimate details about your life and not feel compelled to say, "Please don't tell anyone?"

- Who is the one person who fills a void or need without your having to ask?

- Who is the one person whose hug embraces your spirit as well as your body?

Enter the person's name below after you are satisfied with your qualifying choices.

My Get Me Thru Partner is:

ACTION: Now, you must call the person and ask if they are willing to be your Get Me Thru Partner. Here are a few responses to their anticipated questions:

Question: What is a Get Me Thru Partner?
Answer: A Get Me Thru Partner is someone you trust to know your strengths and weaknesses and your plan of action for living better despite them.

A Get Me Thru Partner is someone who is willing to complete all the exercises you completed to better understand your goals and objectives.
A Get Me Thru Partner is someone who is a friend who loves you as you are, but also wants you to be the best you possible.

Question: Why do you need A Get Me Thru Partner?
Answer: You need a Get Me Thru Partner because it is almost impossible to get thru alone, even though the Stranger is always with you.

Question: How long will you need A Get Me Thru Partner?
Answer: You will need A Get Me Thru Partner for the rest of your life, or until you decide that you no longer desire to get thru.

ACTION: Purchase a copy of The Voice of My Boundaries for your new partner or ask them to purchase one for him/herself. Your **Get Me Thru Partner** is to complete the exercises in the same manner as you did, following all the instructions. You may coach them, but do not perform the work with them. Certainly, let them see your Peaceful Location. Do not share your answers with them until they complete Chapters one thru nine and finalize their Get Me Thru Partner selection. Ideally, they should choose you as their Get Me Thru Partner. Waiting to discover their selection may be difficult, but I assure you it will be worth it.

Chances are you made a poor selection if you discover you were not selected to be their Get Me Thru Partner as well. Start your selection process again. I know that's a disturbing call, but as your Coach I had to make it. However, congratulations if you discover you are their selected Get Me Thru Partner. You may move to the next Action with your new Partner.

ACTION: Exchange books with your partner for a week. Use the week to review each other's notes and to learn more about each other. No one else should be allowed to read the books.

ACTION: Make notes regarding your concerns. Write your surprises and expectations in the space provided for your Partner to read. Focus on anything new and things you expected *to see,* but did not see. Don't hesitate to express your feelings. Remember you are now part of **A Get Me Thru Partnership**.

Action: Secure your partner's book as you secure your own. Return the books at the end of the week and read each other's notes from the exercise.

GET ME THRU PARTNER NOTES:

GET ME THRU PARTNER NOTES:

ACTION: Schedule a time to sit down and discuss your findings, support plans and a time to resume your exercises. Stay on schedule. I will see you in a week!

CHAPTER TEN

DAILY LOVE FOR TOMORROW'S STRENGTH

Congratulations! I hope you and your Get Me Thru Partner affirmed many things and discovered some new ones as well. This next exercise is thought provoking and you will need someone close for balance. If honesty prevails, you both will never be the same.

The title, **Daily Love For Tomorrow's Strength** seemed more appropriate for a romance novel than an exercise to me. Admittedly, I did not see it as an exercise in the beginning. Therefore, I reviewed over sixty pages of my notes searching for clarity. In the end, I followed *the voice of my boundaries*. It guided my writing clarity through an indescribable sense of peacefulness. My peacefulness was sedating and I pray I am able to paint a portrait of it through words in this chapter. There are many inspirations for this exercise and perhaps that is why I had such a difficult time seeing the message clearly. I also attribute my difficulty to the creative symmetry that often leaves me at the doorsteps of inspiring nuggets of wisdom. I enjoy having colorful nuggets unfold into spiritual portraits of inspiration. Likewise, I have been blessed to use many nuggets to give depth to my revelations, but few as intense as this one:

**"I can go to hell for a day,
as long as I know I'm coming back."**

Whew! I learned that one many years ago from someone very dear to me. I thought it was cute back then, but now it is a way of life for me. Life has a way of making you feel like you are visiting hell, until grace and mercy rescue you and allow you to return. The returns have become my sources of wisdom and strength. I have accepted that each return from hell is a gift from God and gifts from God are intended blessings for others. Every time I return from hell I have a debt that I am more than willing to pay. Wow, life really is a cycle! If you receive, you are to give and if you give you are destined to receive more. Why then doesn't it happen more often? Great question and that is what this chapter is all about. It doesn't happen more because many of us fail to love ourselves. The answer is simple, but the resolve is difficult. However, practicing this exercise will help you *to see* through it much better. Learning to love you is not a selfish goal, but an act of wisdom. The Get Me Thru nugget of wisdom that inspired this chapter should help prove it to you.

**"Create reasons daily to love yourself,
for there will be days when others won't remember too."**
GMT #3703

The inspiration includes the who, what, why, and when. It could not be clearer. I believe you would have to practice spiritual blindness not *to see* the point. I did see all of these elements in the beginning, but I did not *see* how to put them into practice every day for the rest of my life. I began by asking myself hundreds of questions. Ask yourself this question aloud, right now.

"Is it easier for me to love someone else than it is for me to love myself?"

I asked myself that question several years ago soon after this nugget was placed in my spirit. My answer was a disturbing yes, as I took each Get Me Thru nugget personally. It was easier for me to live with the shortcomings and secrets of others than it was for me to live with my own. My exceptions for others were always seen by me as nonjudgmental loving acts. However, I expected more from myself and you are probably not much different. Consequently, the standard I held so close to my shortcomings began to threaten my ability of discernment when it came to knowing and loving the real me. It is easy to do, believe me. It is also one of those things that can fly under your spiritual radar. You don't see it developing for the superficial success. Overachievers miss it all the time, because they are constantly moving. Nonetheless, there are few who are immune to such feelings. It is important for you to consider this point early in this exercise, because not knowing who you are misrepresents your value. It also keeps you from seeing the need to love you through daily practices.

"When you fail to know who you are, you make it difficult to love yourself and inevitably increase your visits to hell."

If you are not careful, your visits to hell will result in more withdrawals from your spirit than deposits. Exercising will change that and give you strength in return.

Let's talk about how to create reasons to love you everyday. Everyday is a heavy request, but it only implies there is always something new and rewarding to put into practice. Previously I talked about change, but let's replace it with *new practices*. Change as you learned is intimidating, so from this point, the effective word is *practice*. Read these questions and let them rest in your spirit during this exercise. It is not important to answer them now. Why? – Because my objective for now is to plant a seed of wisdom about questions.

"Questions change the world by inspiring new practices, because questions rest in places of the spirit where answers only visit for a short while."

These questions are personal. You only need one of them to rest in your spirit to get the true meaning. Though several of them inspired me, I will share one that is special to me later. Read these questions as often as you need and until you find that special one.

- Can you remember your first love? I don't mean the first school crush, but your first real love. The one that kept you awake at night dreaming and smiling at sunrise while daydreaming.
- What things did you do to assure the person you cared?
- How did you discover their likes and dislikes?
- How did you stay encouraged to continue your loving acts toward the person?
- How did you address their shortcomings?
- Did fear ever become a part of your relationship?
- Was fear a sign of weakening or a need for some new practices?
- Was your show of love driven by expectations of how you wanted to be loved?
- Did you require others in your life to treat them kindly as well?
- Did you treat yourself better when they were around or worst?
- Did you make personal sacrifices for them?
- Do you believe actions speak louder than words when it comes to love?

- Did you continue to show the person love when it was not reciprocated?
- If your loving acts were not reciprocated, did it cause you to focus more on what your love was costing you?
- Do you believe your love made the other person a better person?
- Did loving the other person make you a better person?
- Did you learn anything about yourself while showing love to the other person?
- Was there ever a point when your love for the person was not enough to keep you moving?
- Did loving the person take away from being you?
- If you are no longer with that person, do you feel you left a piece of yourself with him or her?
- If you answered yes to the above question, how much did the forfeiture cost you?

Remember I am your Coach and I promised you I would not ask you to do anything I have not done or would not do. I therefore have a confession to make. There is one question that started my juices flowing about this exercise. The question is: "Was your show of love driven by expectations of how you wanted to be loved?" My honest answer was *Yes*. What better way to tell a person something than to show them—right? *Yes* is the correct answer, but allow me to clarify it. Using *show to receive* as a guide to love is unfair and not reliable. Though difficult to admit, it is my concession. Loving another person according to your will is no guarantee of their seeing your love as a model to replicate. However, it is easier to love a person who is comfortable enough to love who they are now and who they are becoming. I respect that as a two-way street and it has been emotionally liberating. That resolve enabled me to see why *show to receive* was not the best way to have love reciprocated. The more love and respect you have for *you*, the easier it is to love others without conditions.

Now because of my resolve, it is difficult to love another who stops living their life to become absorbed into my world. Please don't miss this point. What happens after a person steps completely into your world? I'll gladly tell you. The pressure is then on you to preserve enough for you both. You eventually resent the unintended obligation and disrespect will incubate on both sides. Disrespect is a dangerous thing when it comes to love, because it stands on the borders with love and hate. Only time will tell the whole story, but it is as common as rain. I told you that this was going to be a tough exercise.

Essentially, the best way to have strength for tomorrow as the title of this chapter implies, is to practice loving you every day. Practice suggests change and the responses *"impossible and why"* typically follows a request for change. However, what is impossible is to love where there is no self-respect. That is why it is important for you to complete daily practices for you. Others will follow with love in tow, guaranteed. Did I hear you ask, how? I've been waiting for you to ask. I'll give you an answer in three steps:

1. Determine if there is a need to love you better.
2. Identify the missing links.
3. Consider this Get Me Thru nugget of wisdom for inspiration to move forward:

"When we fail to love ourselves, we quickly look to those closest by to hate."

GMT #1709

This nugget is a piercing danger sign. The first person in the line of fire is you and the second is the one closest to you. *Whew!* This happens without fail. Ponder it for a minute. Your strength for tomorrow begins with you!

"Will somebody please say Amen?"

Can you see the danger that develops when you fail to create reasons to love you? You and innocent people suffer. Consider this question. "How difficult is it to stand by and watch someone you love destroying himself or herself?" Very difficult I am sure. What then happens when people fail to love themselves? I have the answer, so please commit it to your spirit. YOU QUICKLY LOOK FOR THOSE CLOSEST BY TO HATE! I was shouting, but without apology. No one wins when you fail to love you. Oh, did I hear you ask, "Why do we seemingly hate those closest by?" Because, it is easy and a sure way to feel empowered. Sincere love is reassuring to the receiver. However, self-depleting sacrifices lessen respect for the giver. It then creates a painful perception of how to love you back. *Whew!* I know that one hurts, but the truth stands. Am I saying this is etched in stone? No, but I am saying it is not far from stone. Examine your own records *to see*. It is not as important for me to be right as it is for you *to see* the inspiration.

Don't put yourself at risk for hate. Protect yourself by creating reasons daily to love yourself. You can be certain there will be days when others won't remember too. The days that others forget to love themselves may be the days you are the closest. You will be safe because of your firm foundation of daily love. On that note, relax and allow me to step away for a few minutes.

I introduced you to my Miss Annie Episode in previous chapters, but I did not give you the details and full impact that it has had on my life. I talk a lot about wisdom episodes because I believe they are also designed to help define the essence of spiritual boundaries. The Miss Annie Episode was certainly the beginning of inspiration and honoring spiritual boundaries for me.

Miss Annie was a very good friend of my MaDear's. In fact, she was part of an extended family in our community network. Everyone knew Miss Annie. Her laugh was thunderous and it made you laugh just to hear it. I was blessed to hear it often as she and MaDear were Club Members and that included the local Sewing Circle, Missionary Society, Eastern Star and Christmas Savings Clubs. The meeting places rotated among the members, which meant Pound Cake and Kool-Aid for sure when our turn came. I was more excited than my brother and sister to have them meet at our house, because the mixing bowl of left over cake batter was always mine. I don't remember why I was so excited about this particular meeting day, but I was very excited. I did not know that a meeting at our home would prove to be life-changing for me.

The specific meeting was The Christmas Savings Club, it was near Christmas and at our home. That was indeed a good combination for me for several reasons. Particularly, it meant I could remind MaDear of what I wanted for Christmas. It was easy and fun, as I believed in Santa Claus far beyond the time limits of my brother and sister. I had a philosophy that to believe was to receive! Well, something began to press on me and I felt compelled to make MaDear aware of it. However, it was unacceptable to interrupt adults during my childhood. It was an understanding rarely breached. I therefore had to wait patiently for the right moment of interjection. I inconspicuously followed Miss Annie and MaDear towards the kitchen. I watched them from behind our dining room door hoping to catch a glimpse of my MaDear's eyes for a nod to speak. The opportunity never happened. I waited and waited and then something else happened. I overheard Miss Annie ask my MaDear the question that introduced me to portions of my boundaries. She said, "Carrie Bell, where did you and Curtis get Dee Dee from —she is the ugliest child you got and she don't look like nobody…?" I didn't cry because I desperately needed to see my MaDear's face. I remember saying to myself as I heard another of Miss Annie's big laughs, "MaDear, please don't laugh." She did not laugh, neither did she see me behind the door. I remember that it was the question that lingered in my spirit— the question and not the answer. I somehow knew I could not change the truth if that was what she saw, but I could address the essence of the question. My processing that incident was clearly that of a child's mind. Nonetheless, I had an opportunity to gain some nuggets of wisdom later that night.

I wasn't able to sleep and I knew MaDear was also awake. There was no hallway between us, just a doorway, so I tapped on the sliding door for permission to enter. She said, "Come in." I found her reading her Bible. I remember walking slowly towards her bed, because I was not certain about how I was going to approach the subject of what I experienced. It was difficult, because as a child I did not know how to say that an adult had done something wrong *and that it hurt me. My resolve was simple and I said, "MaDear, I heard what Miss Annie said about me." Whew! She looked into my eyes and patted the mattress for me to sit beside her, which I did. She then held my face in her hands and said, "You're not ugly baby, you're not ugly." She hugged me, and that is the night that our hearts touched and locked for life. I then looked into her eyes and said, "MaDear, when I grow up I am not going to judge people by the way they look. I am going to get to know people first, because you can't tell how pretty a person is by looking at them..." Whew! God is amazing, for what a seed to plant in the spirit of a child. Can you see how quickly God planted the nugget of wisdom? Though painful, it was the question that opened the door to wisdom. It was not the pain nor the answer, but the question!*

Miss Annie's unintended but painful question caused me not only to look for reasons to love myself, but to look deeply for reasons to love others as well. I am convinced that making your spirit available to God allows wisdom to come through some of the most unlikely episodes. Search your spirit daily for them and I am certain that He will grant you no less.

Miss Annie helped me *to see* that in the end what matters is who you see when you look into the mirror and when you close your eyes. It is a wisdom episode that has given me balance every time I tip my spirituality scales.

"There will always be days when others won't remember to love me, but there should not be days when I forget."

My Miss Annie Episode introduced me to questions for which I did not need answers. Can you see it? If not, please pray that God grants you the vision *to see* it. It is important for you *to see* how questions of tomorrow fit into this exercise. Don't worry because I did not see it in the beginning, but consider this inspiration, which by the way is my favorite from **The Get Me Thru Collection®.**

"My worst and most frightening dream —*is not having one.*"
GMT #2705

Once again, the true complexity in life is accepting its simplicity. It was no accident that this is the nugget that found solace in my spirit. Can you see it? Except I stay focused on always having a dream, I will lose sight of reasons to love me. *Whew!* Essentially, tomorrow is a part of everyone's dream.

"You will either carry-over today's successes for energy or try to erase its failures through the hope of tomorrow's opportunities."

My worst and most frightening dream is not having one, but my faith in God's tomorrow supremely illuminates my pathways and boundaries. It always comes back to boundaries. *Whew!*

On that note, let me step away again before you begin your Actions. My ability to identify nuggets of wisdom is a gift, of that I am certain. I am thankful to God for trusting me to share them. I stepped away this time to give you more examples of nuggets of wisdom. My stepping away also allows me to coach you on an intimate level. Such intimacy is what separates coaching from therapy. I will have failed sadly if I am unable to help you to see wisdom through your episodes. I do not want to fail. More importantly, I do not want you to miss your own nuggets because you think they must be profound. I am convinced that all wisdom has an intended purpose that is often unacknowledged because of misguided expectations. I almost missed my gift because I did not see that it could be linked to wisdom designed to help others. I wanted something profoundly obvious with glittering lights and the works. Isn't that what most children and adults dream of experiencing. Nevertheless, God continued to bless me with more episodes until I began to see His light for me. The light is shining for you as well.

Surely, I could have avoided a few episodes had I acknowledged His gift sooner, but I can't imagine which one nor would I like to know. I am however certain that my Miss Annie Episode was part of my destiny.

On the surface, many of my nuggets of wisdom appear to be succinct. I assure you each nugget is attached to an episode in my life. My having lived each one allows me to simplify and share them with you. Your nuggets of wisdom may well be just for you! You may never have to share them with another human being, other than your Get Me Thru Partner. On the other hand, you too may be called to share them with the world. Consider this Get Me Thru nugget of wisdom, as you are certain to be affected by its message.

"When hate becomes hatred the pain is universal."
GMT #2721

It required a mere thirty-nine letters to form the eight words that helped me *to see* terrorism, racism and war from a completely different perspective. This nugget touched my soul and I had no idea how I would share it. Once again, I did not see how such subject matter would complement inspiration and love of self. I missed it, but how could I have missed something that was so clear? Only God knows and I am glad He decided to reveal it to me. Hate like love dwells within our souls. Therefore, you can't afford to ignore either one because of their common habitat. *Whew!*

Let's examine those eight words for wisdom that I pray will change your life and the lives of those around you. The implication is that hate is embryonic and that hatred's gestation is the dreadful delivery that affects humankind. Hate is one of those weaknesses that fly under the radar of spiritual boundaries. It sits sometimes quietly in your spirit, but it rarely weakens in its stillness. In fact, hate grows more in stillness and quietness. Think back with me to Columbine, Race Riots, and The Oklahoma City Bombing and The World Trade Center tragedies. I challenge you not to find that hate incubated until it became hatred. I believe *hatred is hate in action.* The frightening thing about hatred is you can seldom know its destination until it arrives. Where is the wisdom here? The wisdom is in knowing that we cannot afford to ignore hate. Hate when left alone has the potential to create universal pain. *Whew!* Am I saying wisdom means you should appeal to congress to pass new laws? No, I am not. Am I saying this wisdom means you should become fanatical and try to convince everyone who is different from you that you love them? Absolutely not! I am simply saying that *universal change begins through one heart at a time.* I know you've heard that advice before, but not from this perspective. Remember that change is just another way of saying, *new practices.* The next time someone you know expresses hate, be mindful of the potential of hatred. You may be the one giving an interview one day saying, "I can't believe something like that happened in our community."

"Hate does not necessarily seek out particular people; instead it seeks quiet weakened spirits for growth."

Can you believe all that and more came from eight little words? I am careful today how I use the word hate and more mindful of how those around me use it. Remember, *one spirit at a time*. Guess what, sometimes hate will find a haven in your spirit if you don't practice creating reasons to love you. This nugget of wisdom on hate deserves your personal attention. It should be easy *to see* that hatred demands a huge audience for each of its deliveries to humankind. Once you give life to hate it seeks to control your entire being. It will also seek to destroy your desire to hear *the voice of your boundaries*. You can't afford to hesitate or concede, especially when it comes to creating reasons to love you, so don't miss the point. The opposite of love is still hate and you thought I was talking about other people.

I believe hate is also a tool for profit and advancement. It often begins with self-induced fear, which is why it is imperative for you to create reasons daily to love yourself. Remember acts of hatred like love does bring people together, but unlike love hatred cannot keep people together. Why? — Because fear sets in and divides, but you can change that with *new practices*.

Consider this final point about hate and fear. I don't believe hate was the initial driving force behind introducing slavery in America. However, I am convinced that slavery was an act of laziness and greed. There was no logical basis for the hate between people who were worlds apart in nearly every aspect. Actually, hate came later and then hatred followed. However, once implemented, it was the fear of loss of profit and laziness that created breeding grounds for hate. Eventually hatred infected the spirit of the slave masters. It sadly divided God's family through generations to come. Don't miss this point and suffer a tangent about slavery. This is about how fear can become your spiritual nemesis when you fail to create reasons to love you. Fear is a destructive power in the hands of the wrong people. I believe that spiritual fear of God is the beginning of wisdom. So, if you desire spiritual wisdom, your fear should rest in God. I realize this perspective may appear awkward here, but it is just what you need to reckon with reasons to love yourself. Misguided fear will cause you to stand still and rob you of growth opportunities designed to yield respect and love. Don't allow fear to find refuge in your spirit for very long. Ponder this perspective and monitor your spirituality radar accordingly. I will clarify *fear* in detail for you in Chapter Twelve. It is from a perspective that you do not want to miss!

I have also learned that nuggets of wisdom will cause you to think on levels you never considered. I once believed happiness was something I could possess and have for a lifetime. My MaDear taught me to be smart in school, get a good education, a good job and to be happy. I did all she taught me with one exception. Capturing happiness was like chasing the wind. I could feel its presence near, but it always seemed to get around me or above me somehow. My concentration became spiritually blinding until one day I made an appeal to God. I was willing to take whatever I could get at that point, as both of my parents were deceased, the fertility God had chosen not to show me favor, I had buried a husband in the name of peace and was once near death's door myself. My appeal left me with this nugget of wisdom:

"Happiness comes fleetingly, affording you no time to waste, and it is then that seconds will represent lifetimes."

GMT #3708

Everything I had been praying for was answered in that nugget, but I did not see it before my appeal to God. Happiness was indeed like the wind, which is why I could not expect it to linger nor wait on me. Wisdom teaches me to enjoy my happiness, for it is divinely fleeting to bless our spirit with many lifetime memories. Remember the nugget I shared with you about one of us being left with memories? I now look forward to my happiness resting in the memories that are forming my life.

I have gained peacefulness that allows me to speak boldly of my spiritual episodes as nuggets of wisdom. Accordingly, I have another nugget that has touched my life and the lives of most people I know. This may be the one to release you *to see* everything that is for you and it is simple:

GMT #1717

"When the past blocks your view of the future – you have an enemy within."

I hope this nugget hits home for you like it did for me. Pause with me for a moment. Close your eyes and just think back to times when your past kept you standing still. You and only you knew the real reason, while others could only guess why. I have found that every nugget of wisdom I have received directs me to look within for answers and even more deeply for questions. Each time the questions have proven to be more powerful than the answers, because the questions became inspiration. Let's see how many questions this nugget disclosed to me.

1. How can I move forward and not see the future?
2. What does my past have to do with it?
3. What part of my past is at issue?
4. Why can't I go forward despite the issue?
5. How long has my past been holding me back?
6. How many opportunities have I missed because of my blindness?
7. Who or what is the enemy?
8. How long has the enemy been there?

9. How can I get the enemy out?
10. How can I make sure the enemy never returns?
11. Does anyone else know about my enemy?
Have you ever wondered why you can't seem to get going, or why you quit too soon, or why you are content with mediocrity? You may have an enemy within. If so, exercise some spring-cleaning and start creating reasons to love you through your own nuggets of wisdom. Indulge me these final two nuggets before you begin to work.

"Sometimes standing still keeps you moving."
GMT #3704

Stand still for a few minutes, as you are about to exercise a level of spirituality that may lead you into unfamiliar waters. I have given you much to ponder and don't want to overwhelm you. Therefore, now would be a good time to practice whatever gives you a sense of peace. It may be a silent prayer, a warm shower or bath, the scent of a candle, your favorite song, a short walk or simply closing your eyes for a few minutes. Start practicing various techniques now and use them whenever you feel a need to release. Don't be surprised if a few of your nuggets cause you to experience an open release of tears. I guarantee you that most of them will not be tears of sadness, but of cleansing. Here is your final nugget for this exercise. I have chosen not to expound on it, as it speaks for itself.

"My tears and I have an understanding—I promise not to let them build up and they promise not to push. In return, I am cleansed and they get relief."
GMT #1712

Again, I step away during your exercises to grant you a vicarious view of how I have reckoned with the voice of my own boundaries. It is now time for you and your partner to step away.

ACTION: Write about two recent Wisdom Episodes familiar to you and your Get Me Thru Partner. One is your episode and one is your partner's episode. You are to write about them in detail. It does not matter if you both were a part of the episode. It does matter that you are aware of it. Only write about a previously written episode if it is your *Ms. Annie Episode*. Understand that you are expected to write about your own episode and your partner's episode. You must agree on the episodes and not select them independently. This is a growth Action designed to help you *see* the perspective of your own spirituality. Your perspective will come through your eyes as well as the eyes of your partner.

Consider the following points in making your selection:

- Is there evidence the episode affected your life?
- Is there something you have not discussed that would make a difference?
- Is there something positive to be gained from writing about the episode?
- Is there something in the episodes that will strengthen your partnership?

Also, your episodes should reveal evidence reflective of how you treated yourself after the episode. That is to say, is there evidence of wisdom that inspires you to create reasons daily to love you better?

ACTION: Step away from this exercise for at least a day before writing about the episode.

Your Recent Wisdom Episode:

Your Partner's Recent Wisdom Episode:

ACTION: Exchange books with your partner for at least three to five days. Read both episodes aloud in your Peaceful Location. Look for honesty and areas where you can give support and clarity. This is not about criticism, but about support and wisdom.

ACTION: Schedule at least a couple of hours to meet and discuss your discoveries. The location should be quiet and outside your respective Peaceful Locations. I could not let you go without sharing this last priceless nugget.

"It takes knowledge to love someone else, but it takes wisdom to create reasons to love yourself and courage to do it every day."

Many blessings as you carry out one of your most defining and caring exercises…

A Get Me Thru Nugget of Wisdom:

"A testimony about your experiences, both good and bad
is a lighted pathway for those who follow."

CHAPTER ELEVEN

FINANCIAL SPIRITUALITY AND WELLNESS

Welcome to the **Financial Spirituality and Wellness** exercise! I admit finance and exercising are not typically approached from a spirituality perspective. However, financial peace of mind is as much about exercising spiritual resolve as any subject presented so far. In fact, the characteristics and practices that compromise or promote personal, professional and physical wellness are the same for financial wellness. You stayed with me this far, so hear me out. I have a few more plays you might enjoy running. Let's begin with a simple question about financial wellness.

How many times have you said, "I just want to help people?" Many times I'm sure. If I had a ten-dollar bill for every time I said it, I could feed and clothe several families. As a child, *helping people* was one of my mantras. The more my family needed, the more I wanted to grow up faster and help other people. The reality of my youthful desires hit me much later.

I learned the reality of help is *money*. Verbal heartfelt givers will not like that concession, but it is true. It is called *emotional support* when you don't have money to give and *help* when you do have money to give. That understanding only comes through the gateway of financial spirituality, which comes from wisdom. Allow me to say, money is not evil and I am thankful that it isn't, since everyone on earth needs it. However, your perspective of money sets the stage for evilness with money, but it is not because of money. *Will somebody please say Amen!*

Some would say that combining finance and spirituality is like mixing religion and politics. I disagree, because religions are based on selected doctrines and denominations with many of man's selfish influences. Likewise, politics is designed with man's selfishness for the advantage of a select few. The fair practice of religion and politics is not available to everyone, while universal spirituality is available to everyone who accepts it. Spirituality fits into every aspect of life. Spirituality is the essence of our creation. Spirituality is the essence of goodness that allows people to love one another. Spirituality separates man from beast. Spirituality is God within you that helps you keep religion in its proper perspective. Spirituality is what separates risk takers from contentment and humankind fearfulness. Spirituality speaks to you and does not allow others to hear. Religions can learn a lot from spirituality.

I was told once, the reason capable people don't have financial peace of mind is because they are not willing to do what it takes to earn it. That is simple enough and it is true. This is a good time to remember the two facts about time we discussed earlier. Go back to them on page 127 if you can't remember them. Your financial peace of mind is at stake.

Having financial peace of mind is like wanting to go to heaven. Most people want to go to heaven, but it's the dying that stops them from raising their hands to go today. Likewise, most people want financial peace of mind. However, the sacrifice, risk, opportunity, preparation, wisdom, common sense, gift, talent, diligent work and spiritual resolve stands between them. It is not just *time*, because everyone has the same amount, so it must be something else.

You are probably still wondering why I included a chapter on Financial Spirituality. I did so because we live in a society where almost everything is a function of money.

•Living is a function of money.

•Retirement is a function of money and not necessarily of time.

•Dying is a function of money.

•Sickness is a function of money.

•Eating is a function of money.

•Health is a function of money.

•Education is a function of money.

•Love in its own way is a function of money and that is someone else's book I'm sure. The list is endless, but you get the picture. You can't even worship without someone spending some money and you certainly can't give... *Whew!*

The function of money is a unique matter. You can move beyond its preset limits only if you listen to *the voice of your boundaries*. Financially successful people have mastered surpassing the limits. They are clearly driven by something from within. Don't miss the point.

There are secrets to financial spirituality that most people fearfully avoid. The secret to financial spirituality is the level of faith you exercise through *the voice of your boundaries.* Once again, we are back to that powerful voice within you. I am convinced that every human being is destined to experience a measure of financial success. Caution, I am not talking about praying to God and waiting on a miracle. That is a movie script and not a **Get Me Thru** perspective. God expects far more from you than just a prayer. The implication that prayer is all you need is an excellent example of a religious doctrine. As a child, I often heard people say, "All I need is God." I disagree. I need God and my fellowman. The goodness and mercifulness of God is revealed through the lives of human beings created in His image. That was the plan from the start. However, I admit we are not following through as well as He intended. Don't shoot the messenger, because my goal is to leave you thinking. I hope my honesty causes you to think beyond my words.

A business associate of mine experienced great financial success in a network marketing business. In fact, he became a millionaire many times over. He shared with me that as his money increased, so did the criticism about him and what he was doing with it. Most of the criticism was from his brother,— a brother who was unwilling to pay the price for his own financial peace of mind. My associate had no audience, as it was just he and I. His words landed in my spirit and there they remain. He said, *"Dee Dee, I told my brother at least I'm willing to do more than just enough to feed my own family. I can help others without taking away from my family. But, you are too lazy and will only do enough for you and your family. How selfish is that?"* He admitted that the exchange left him feeling cleansed and he no longer felt guilty about his financial peace of mind. Financial resolve requires you to see beyond what already is and into dreams of peacefulness. It is about perspective. *Can you see it?*

Consider this, money is a medium of exchange and not just change! To get money, you must exchange your knowledge, labor, or a product. It is just that simple. However, each will have self-imposed limitations, once you decide not to exercise them. Do I expect to experience Financial Peace of Mind someday? You better believe I do! I will die expecting it or die knowing I achieved it. Either way, I will not stand still waiting on it. Can you see it? This may surprise you, but there will always be more than enough money,— *the government prints money.* Your challenge is to earn your share. You must have a plan and a winner's perspective on which to build and grow to earn your share. You are never too young or too old once a proper perspective is in place. I was born in 1954 and in 2004, **The Voice of My Boundaries** delivered me as a new born baby. I am just getting started, and so can you. Remember, value is added to money after the government prints it! *Whew!*

Spend time cultivating your gift. There is value in every God-given gift. However, it is only available to you through your spiritual resolve. Many people say, "I will be happy when I discover my gift." Look inside! Spend time with *you* and your gift will come through as an image in a mirror. Don't forget that the value is in your gift. You are as a hidden treasure and you have the map. *So, how do you tap into your financial spirituality using your gift?* I can only inspire you with an outline and nuggets of wisdom. You must develop the plan or it isn't your plan.

"Every capable individual should seek financial independence for peace of mind. However, financial independence is not a guarantee of peacefulness."

Peacefulness comes in having a spiritual resolve about your financial wellness. If you do not exercise financial spirituality, you cannot expect to have financial independence. In the end, your life can become one vicious cycle. This is one of those simple, but not easy situations to exercise.

I had little spiritual regard for my financial wellness and professional success before I began to listen to *the voice of my boundaries*. I only applied spirituality to those things I thought were respectable church religious matters. I applied spirituality to my health, religion and to my family relationships. I did not have the wisdom to know that spirituality was a universal matter. Don't get me wrong. I prayed about everything, but not from a spiritual perspective. My prayers for financial wellness were from a perspective of need. I was willing to work hard for the rest. I depended on my relationship with God for necessities and me for the luxuries. I have learned that it was an unnecessary division. I thought if I couldn't take it to church it was my problem. I didn't accept that it didn't have to go anywhere, and that God had placed His voice within me to guide me to the finish line. My MaDear started that ball to rolling by making sure I learned to put things in my head where no one else could take it away. However, it took a personal relationship with the Spirit of my being to convince me a universal application was also expected. I do not want to over simplify spirituality, but it is simple. Check the statements you have uttered or heard someone else say or gestures you made.

☐ "Lord, help me!" (My favorite prayer)
☐ "Oh, my God!"
☐ "It worked out somehow...!"
☐ "Give me just a minute..." (While closing your eyes tightly and thinking)
☐ Shake your finger searching for a thought
☐ "If it's God's will..."
☐ Close your eyes to meditate
☐ "I can't believe I did that..."

Everything I just described is an indication of a spiritual acknowledgement.

"Spirituality is supreme, because no man can say he has experienced its limits."

That is why I am convinced that to apply spirituality to the *whole of life* is the key. Actually, spirituality is one of the most comprehensive words known to man, because through it God can be a part of every aspect of you. Let's do a little work to measure your application of spiritual resolve.

ACTION: Rate your spiritual resolve about five important components of life. Namely, your success in health, family, financial wellness, career and religion. Place an "X" in the appropriate section. *HINT: The voice of your boundaries is a clear indicator of spiritual regard; especially when you fail to listen.*

	Spiritually Strong	Spiritually Weak	Financial Considerations
Religion			
Health			
Family			
Career			
Financial			

Answer this question, are you strong in all areas? If not, join the club. My experience is that not one person can honestly say they are strong in all areas. I did not include *average,* because to be spiritually average is a misleading sense of contentment. The goal however, is to start applying spirituality to all of them. Did you just ask,— How can I? Okay, I saw that one coming, so here is an answer. Which areas did you rate Spiritually Strong and were your ratings honest? If yes, great!

Remember I said a few chapters back you held the answers within? You do and now I can prove it to you. If you were honest and rated just *one* area as Spiritually Strong, you already have a successful plan in place. You clearly have daily practices in place that are working for you. The problem with areas rated Spiritually Weak maybe that you have limited your practices to specific areas as I did. In all likelihood, you have been hitting and missing, and while the hitting has been enough to carry you, it is a dangerous practice for financial wellness.

I use the term wellness as a matter of perspective. I now see financial wellness in the same light of physical wellness. Deep down I know when I haven't done something, could have done something, or should have done something. My body alerts me. I have a choice to honor it or to neglect it. It is no different with financial wellness. You know when something is wrong and I'm not talking about your bank account alone. I am talking about the actions before the bank account. *Whew!*

Everything you have exercised so far fits into this exercise: *Who you are, why you are who you are, where you are in life, how you love you, how you process changes, whether you honor your boundaries and your spiritual resolve.* Each one plays a role in your perspective about your financial wellness. I pray you see it.

Let's discuss a word that inevitably comes up when talking about financial peace of mind—*entrepreneur*. Most people believe you must work for yourself to experience *financial peace of mind.* In a small measure, I agree. I also believe a new perspective will help more people to experience success than have in the past. You do not have to be an entrepreneur to benefit from its purpose, which is to create income outside the boundaries of standard employment. If you are not an entrepreneur, don't say that you are and do not accept others labeling you as one. On the other hand, if you need more money, you must call it something. It may be a second job or even a third. Being an entrepreneur is rewarding, but it is also intimidating and not for the faint at heart.

- True entrepreneurs are different and rarely content. They provide employment for themselves and others, while accepting the obligations and risks. No doubt, accepting risk is what separates the faithful from the faithless and the strong from the weak. Nonetheless, consider the added benefits if you learn how to apply an entrepreneur's perspective to your financial way of life. Learn how to think like an entrepreneur and you will exercise a higher level of financial resolve. There are many valuable lessons to learn from an entrepreneur, even if you never become one.
- Entrepreneurs position themselves to learn new things.
- Every entrepreneur has a valuable Wisdom Episode to share.

- Entrepreneurs are told *no* more times than they are told *yes*.
- Entrepreneurs make excellent mentors.
- Entrepreneurs are not afraid of being afraid.
- Entrepreneurs wake-up early in the morning.
- Entrepreneurs associate with successful people.
- Entrepreneurs fall down often and get up often.
- Entrepreneurs laugh at themselves.
- Entrepreneurs enjoy the fruits of their labor.

I have many successful friends who are excellent employees, but lousy entrepreneurs in spirit. They resist change and prefer being micro-managed. There is nothing wrong with their choice. Financial wellness is still available to them and to you. However, you must learn to apply some of the entrepreneurial characteristics. It is a matter of perspective, whether you are an entrepreneur or employee. Consider these questions.

- Do you believe you can achieve financial wellness?
- Do you believe you deserve financial wellness?
- Do you accept that your financial wellness and physical wellness need similar attention from you?
- Do you accept that *perspective is about daily practices*?
- Do you believe spiritual resolve about financial wellness can change your life?
- Do you believe the voice that drives you to one success in life can also drive you to all other successes?

I believe the empowering answers are in your application of universal spirituality. Don't just apply it here, but apply it there and there and there. Can you see it? Let's do some more work on your application. Remember, if you checked just one life component as Spiritually Strong on page 197, you have a plan in place. Select one of them for the next Action and perform the Action accordingly.

ACTION: Prepare a daily practice plan using the component of life you rated Spiritually Strong. A Daily Practice Plan is simply a log of your daily practices during a specific matter. Only list practices you exercise daily.

DAILY PRACTICE PLAN

Monday:
Tuesday:
Wednesday:
Thursday:
Friday:
Saturday:
Sunday:

ACTION: Go back to the chart on page 197 and put an "X" by anything that does not require financial considerations.

Chances are, you will not check off an area, if you are honest. Let's go back to my point about common sense for a moment. *"Do you think for one minute, God would allow something as significant as finance to be attached to everything known to man and not have it be a part of His plan of spirituality?" Whew!* Don't miss this point, because I am not talking about riches, fame and fortune only. I am talking about financial peace of mind through spiritual resolve. You may not need a million dollars for financial peace of mind, or a half million dollars or even a quarter of a million dollars and then you may need ten million dollars. I have no way of knowing, but you should know.

"I am certain of one thing. Spiritual resolve includes having financial peace of mind and a continuous relationship with the voice of your boundaries for peacefulness."

It is important that you see the relevance of your financial spirituality. Don't fall for the cute clichés that quitters cling to such as, "Money can't buy you happiness."—"Money isn't everything" or "Money can't buy you love." All of those statements are correct. However, the right answers don't always represent *the spirituality of truth.*

- Yes, money can't buy you happiness, but *truth is*— it buys you time and peace of mind to work on it.
- Yes, money isn't everything, but *truth is*— nearly everything is affected by money.
- Yes, money can't buy you love, but *truth is*—money makes it a lot easier to pursue love. *Truth is*—it also affords you time to learn more about how not to be compromised by a desperation for love.

The essence of this exercise is your spirituality affects every aspect of your life, which includes your financial wellness. That is the whole truth! Remember there must also be balance even to experience the moments of fleeting happiness destined for you. You can no longer afford to nurture your health, family and religion without also nurturing financial spirituality. The same voice that directs your pathways to good health and faithfulness is the same voice that can guide you to *financial peace of mind.*

ACTION: Perform this exercise if you do not have financial peace of mind. I could have designed an impressive spreadsheet, but you don't need an impressive chart. Answer the short questions and then perform the rest of the Action. This exercise is a simple view of your perspective on financial wellness.

1. How much more money per month do you need to have peace of mind?

$_____________

2. If you need more, do you have a plan to get it?

Yes _____ **No** ________

3. Are you afraid to do what it takes to have financial peace of mind?

Yes _____ **No** ________

4. Are you financially healthy?

Yes _____ **No** ________

ACTION: Shade in the entire Smiling Model if you have Financial Peace of Mind. Shade in the entire Sad Model if you Do Not Have Financial Peace of Mind yet. It is important that you shade in the entire model, because you are either happy or you are not. Did I hear you say, *"But Coach, I am comfortable where I am."* If you are comfortable where you are, your model should be smiling and there is no need for a *but*. *Can you see it?*

I Have Financial Peace of Mind

I Do Not Have Financial Peace of Mind

Indulge me this point please. A spiritual reckoning opens your life to all God has for you. I don't believe anyone will live long enough to receive all God has in store for man. Oh, you don't agree, but what if I am right? Can you imagine how much more you stand to receive just by believing you can't use up all your intended blessings? Answer these questions.

1. Are you paid what you believe you are worth? If not, do you have a plan to make up the difference?
   Yes____ **No____**
   Yes, I Have a Plan____ **No, I Do Not Have a Plan____**

2. Do you believe you deserve to be paid what you are worth?
   Yes___ **No___** **Never Considered It___**

3. Would receiving what you are worth give you financial peace of mind?
   Yes___ **No___** **Never Considered It___**

4. Is peace of mind important to you?
Yes___ **No___** **Never Considered It___**

5. What area of your life would be most affected if you had financial peace of mind?

___

___

___

6. Do you agree that money was never meant to stand still?
Yes___ **No___** **Never Considered It___**

7. Is there a specific reason why your financial position is not where you want it to be?

___

___

8. Write down 5 things that could change the direction of your financial well-being and move you closer to peace of mind?

1. ___
2. ___
3. ___
4. ___
5. ___

9. Draw a line through the answers in question 8 that you cannot control.

10. Write down the answers you did not draw a line through.

___

___

___

___

ACTION: Meditate on the answers you have for question 10.

ACTION: Develop a plan of daily practices for each change you did not draw a line through. Follow your plan according to your spiritual resolve. Your financial peace of mind is relative, because it comes back to perspective, honesty and action.

I wish I could wave a magic wand and shower you with spiritual resolve about your financial wellness, but I cannot. Instead, here are more nuggets for you to consider.

- If procrastination has caused you to fail in other areas of your life, it will also affect your financial wellness.
- If misguided fear has caused you to fail in other areas of your life, it will also affect your financial wellness.
- If dishonesty has caused you to fail in other areas of your life, it will also affect your financial wellness.
- If a lack of preparation has caused you to fail in other areas of your life, it will also affect your financial wellness.
- If jealousy has caused you to fail in other areas of your life, it will also affect your financial wellness.
- If self-pity has caused you to fail in other areas of your life, it will also affect your financial wellness.
- If laziness has caused you to fail in other areas of your life, it will also affect your financial wellness.

Remember I talked to you about lazy people? Lazy people will never experience financial peace of mind —never! If you fall into that category, change your perspective now. If you are not lazy, you need to work on your other daily practices. *Is it going to be challenging?* Yes, it is going to be challenging.

My new daily practices include selling a specific number of books. Excuses are unacceptable and I have penalties in place. **The Voice of My Boundaries** guided me to this place in my life. Now, I am depending on it to get me through to *financial peace of* *mind.* It is only right to hold your voice accountable when you listen to its wisdom. I have great expectations about my financial wellness and you should about yours as well.

"Money is not evil, but sometimes not having enough causes good people to do evil things."

Sadly, we attribute evilness with money to wealthy people. It is a cop-out perspective! I applaud those who have achieved financial wellness. I pray they exercise the wisdom to use it wisely while enjoying it.

ACTION: Review your questions and responses with your Get Me Thru Partner and compare your spiritual resolve for Financial Wellness. You just may discover a financial partnership…

ACTION: Secure your book and pencil. Many blessings and I hope you too believe Financial Peace of Mind willing comes through your spirit.

CHAPTER TWELVE

MOTIVATION AND INSPIRATION

Welcome back for the final time and congratulations on seeing your program to the end. The final chapter is a run for victory and is every Coach's dream. It is an opportunity to pull everything together. It is also a time to say *great job*, even though I have no way of knowing how well you performed. Therefore, I pray you benefited from each exercise and your honesty prevailed.

I hope you can see victory in the title of this chapter. I meditated on it often because it is my last opportunity to be with you. I was torn between being over-the-top with motivation and understating with inspiration. I decided the most worthwhile pathway was to give you my revelations of both, as I believe them to be inseparable. A perspective I hope you too will embrace. In fact, motivation, inspiration, hope, and wisdom make up the spirituality that creates the *whole of life*. However, each one is linked to hope and must work together for growth and strength. All that you exercised so far included them. If I have coached you properly, you should have experienced motivation and inspiration throughout this book. If not, expect this chapter to make up for it, because I will not accept defeat. That was purely motivational!

I discovered years ago that most people depend largely on motivation alone as a driving force to success. Many of them fail by quitting and never know the reason why. It is therefore important to keep motivation and inspiration in a linked perspective. Why?—Because motivation alone is a deal breaker that misrepresents hope.

"Motivation and inspiration prepares your spirit to embrace hope and then teaches you how to exercise possibility through wisdom."

On that note, let me step away and tell you about a pitfall in relying on motivation alone:

"There was an old woman who was unable to attend worship services even though she lived a short distance from the church. She sat on her front porch every Sunday to listen as others worshipped. One particular Sunday the praise and singing was unusually loud and enthusiastic. She could not wait for someone to pass by so she could ask about the sermon. Finally, three women approached her house still obviously excited about the worship. She shouted to them, "How was church today?" One replied, "Oh, it was great!" The old woman smiled and said, "Please tell me, what was the sermon about today?" One of the women looked at the old woman in astonishment and said, "I don't know what the sermon was about, but I tell you that man can preach!" The three women walked away as excited as before. Motivation alone did not allow them *to see* inspiration in the sermon. You cannot afford to rely on motivation alone if you expect *to see* hope manifested and wisdom exercised.

I have talked to you about many things. Any one of them has the potential to change your life. However, if I bottled my drive, nuggets of wisdom and faith and poured them over you, it would not be the same for you. I know vicarious experiences can only take you so far. That is why I appeal to you to accept my perspectives on universal spirituality and boundaries. I believe strongly in them and I am committed to sharing them for as long as God allows me. The relationship between motivation and inspiration is so important for your journey. Consider this point.

Motivation is meritorious, but it should never be used alone or as a replacement for inspiration. *I believe motivation alone represents calculated experiences of euphoria that requires physical and emotional energy from the giver and the recipient.* Motivation alone can be exhausting. Inspiration, on the other hand, is just the opposite. Inspiration offers peacefulness and permanency and together they equal wisdom. Inspiration also provides the spirit nourishment that motivation itself requires, but does not yield. Think back to the last time you were motivated by someone else. How long did the motivation last? Let me help you. Chances are, if you attended a rally with a motivational speaker it lasted through the meal you ate immediately afterwards. However, if the speaker was really good you bought a book and tapes and listened to at least half of the tape set.

Motivation is also a profitable marketing tool that is here to stay. I use the word marketing for perspective sake. First, motivation alone is a power word that gets people excited about what's going to happen. It rarely disappoints in that aspect. The agenda for motivational speakers and their seminars is succinct—to leave you enthused and wanting more. You can expect to hear buzz words and chants that raise your adrenaline and stories that empty the reservoir of your tears. The overwhelming fact is, motivation alone can leave you drained with little left for you. You must give much of yourself to create the euphoric environment that most people enjoy. However, when motivation is balanced with inspiration you are not drained, but spiritually energized toward wisdom. Think back for a moment to your last motivational experience and consider these questions.

• **Did you pay to attend?** If so, you made an investment. Most people spend money with expectations of a reasonable return. It is a matter of perspective and I can prove it. A tangible is looked on as a purchase, because of the obvious opportunity to own the item. However, information is looked upon as an investment, as the results are unknown. *Can you see it?* Similarly, when you invest in motivational experiences, you should also expect a measurable return. Sadly, most people leave motivational experiences believing the experience was the product—wrong! Motivation alone requires great energy, so staying there long and often is not recommended. However, everyone can use a jolt now and then and still receive tremendous benefits. I uncovered a couple of secrets about motivation that I call Get Me Thru Motivation Tips:

1. Determine an agenda for yourself before paying to attend a motivational event. An agenda is simply a statement of your needs and expectations from the experience.
2. Focus on your agenda throughout the experience and monitor the measurable results.
3. Always set a date of no longer than two weeks to review your benefits or disappointments. Did you gain or did you lose by attending?

• **Were you required to participate in anyway?** If so, you added to the success of the event. Motivation alone is typically a high-energy event with most of the energy coming from the attendees. I love it, but it can be exhausting. You must therefore keep it in the perspective of jolts tempered for inspiration. I am convinced that motivation is the well-intended companion of inspiration. However, it moves you so fast and so high that you can miss the inspiration by focusing on getting down safely. Perhaps that's why so many people need a rest after being motivated. You should participate and expect to be taken higher and higher, but don't come down empty-handed. This is also why the relationship between motivation and inspiration is so important to your spirituality. Accepting the two as a unit changes your perspective altogether. You will no longer settle for motivation without inspiration.

**"Inspiration is like questions—
it always finds space in your spirit!"**

- **Did you present a personal agenda to the presenter?** If not, you still should have expected to receive long-term benefits. Motivational speakers are paid to excite you and it is your responsibility to extract from their messages accordingly. It would be great if everyone's personal agenda could be addressed, but that only happens in personal sessions. Don't forget your agenda and don't expect others to remember it. The insurance policy is on you and underwritten by you.
- **How long did you remain motivated by the information you received?** The answer has the potential to pay big dividends, so here is a clue.

**"Motivation alone requires nourishment that only
inspiration and wisdom can provide."**

I began this section by telling you motivation is a profitable marketing tool. It is and it generates hundreds of millions of dollars in sales every year. The lure of motivation fills the seats in arenas, moves books and tapes and captures mega television audiences. It is also generous, as it allows you to take as much from it as you possibly can. The key is you must take it, because the industry's number one goal is to package it subliminally for your repeated consumption. Keep motivation in its proper perspective and it will yield high returns for you through the inspiration that it ignites. However, you must exercise discernment with the counterparts of motivation.

An exciting and dangerous counterpart is clichés, which often set the stage for motivation. I bought into a cliché while attending a motivation rally in Dallas, Texas. People were jumping up and down as the speaker recited one rousing cliché after the other. One in particular caught my attention, "F-E-A-R is an acronym that means, **F**alse **E**ducation **A**ppearing **R**eal!" I repeated that for years and I was wrong. That misguided perspective cost me time and money, because it did not yield wisdom for manifesting Hope. The cliché had style, but little substance for spiritual growth. He used the right words to excite people, but he exercised the wrong perspective to yield inspiration and wisdom. His definition of fear blocked the gateway to wisdom. It did not offer an alternative. Instead, it represented a scare tactic that excited people. Can you imagine being educated only to discover that it wasn't real? I know a literal approach was not his intent. Nevertheless, the acronym is not sound for inspiration and wisdom. Fear is legitimate and the right perspective of fear should offer a gateway to inspiration and wisdom. Emotional fear is real and not accepting that fact is unrealistic. However, the speaker failed to tell the crowd that there are two types of fear. One is emotional fear and the other is spiritual fear. One is frightening and the other is comforting. One causes you to stand still while the other prepares you to move forward.

The need for a new perspective became apparent to me after I began to exercise universal spirituality. I discovered the need for a different foundation regarding fear. I accepted that FEAR of God is the foundation for inspiration and wisdom. Stay with me, because once again this is not about religion, but about spirituality. I did not accept it easily because I did not see the merit in a fearfully compelled concession. Therefore, I prayed and asked for clarification of FEAR and here it is as I received it.

Faithful
Exercises
Acknowledging
Reverence

This type of fear as you can see, opens the spirit to Inspiration, Wisdom and Hope. Fear also plays an intrinsic role in the *whole of life* perspective. Fear offers a perspective that can empower you! I hope you see it. Be sure to pick up these nuggets about fear. I want them to land in your spirit.

- You must have faith
- You must exercise faith
- You must acknowledge your faith
- You must show your reverence to God through your faith

I use fear as fuel for my spirituality. It is not frightening, but encouraging. Can you see the power in this perspective?

Allow me to step away again. *I watched the television program "Lost in Space" as a child. The Robinson family was marooned in outer space and lived there accordingly. Young Will Robinson had a robot as a pet. Whenever something threatening approached young Will the robot shouted, "Danger Will Robinson, danger!" Motivation is the robot when it comes to igniting inspiration. When you become excited and motivated, an announcement is also made to your spirit that says, "Get ready, and prepare for inspiration and wisdom!" That is the point at which you must pause and listen to hear the inspiration that leads first to FEAR and then to wisdom. Wisdom will then release your spirit to recognize hope and possibilities. Can you see that?*

Also, motivation alone has a calculated shelf life because it is a marketing tool. You show me a marketing tool that is not designed to keep you coming back and I will show you motivation that has a partnership with inspiration to keep you moving.

Allow me now to focus on my favorite part of this wonderful duo, which is inspiration. I believe *inspiration is a spiritual reception of energy that positions the spirit to receive seeds of wisdom.* Inspiration comes into your life from various sources. Unlike motivation, inspiration isn't just packaged and sold. Granted, inspirational products are sold, but the truth is, inspiration is a gift. You can't see inspiration and you only know where it lands by its manifestation through your life. Inspiration is spiritual evidence and not a purchased miracle product. On that note, let me step away again for a couple of minutes.

By now you should know my MaDear is one of my cherished sources of inspiration. I say is even though she is deceased, because so much of what she lived remains a huge part of my life. It is not just vicarious, but inspiring. I have often wondered why as a child, did so much of what she said to me remain in my spirit. Honestly, I repeated her nuggets of wisdom even as a child. It certainly was not because I was a model child. I assure you I received my share of time at the end of a green switch. A switch by the way, was what MaDear used to whip me. It was a physical attention getter, but it was MaDear's words that held my attention more. Her words always left me thinking even when I didn't think they made sense. I later realized she purposely infused every conversation with reasons to make me think. I don't know if it was because I was her 'why child' or because I didn't ask 'Why?' enough.

My MaDear worked hard at establishing traditions in our home and one was playing the word game, Scrabble®. Her love for words was always fascinating to me considering she only had a sixth grade education. Whew! I learned to enjoy playing it and became very competitive. Consequently, things had the potential to grow intense.

Intense is a mild description of a game between us during the summer of my junior year in college. The intensity required that we play with a mandated dictionary for those who made up words. I was definitely not above doing such a thing. I rarely won a call by deferring a play to the dictionary. On the other hand, MaDear never lost a play because of the dictionary. Nevertheless, I challenged her one time too many. Of course, my challenge proved to be unjustified, but that was not the nugget of wisdom I gained. The word I challenged was beyond me and I unwisely placed the limitation on MaDear. I said to her, "MaDear, I'm in college and I didn't even know that word." She looked at me for a precious few seconds and said,

"DeAtri, there's enough that you don't know to make a whole new world. If you live to be one hundred years old, there will still be enough that you don't know to make a whole new world everyday."

I never forgot her words or the gracious wisdom. Her words were seeds that became a part of my spirit. I pray God's wisdom will give them continuous nourishment for you as well. Motivation alone would have lingered but for a while. She inspired me!

Once again, inspiration is manifested in the most unlikely experiences. One specific experience nearly cost me the opportunity to deliver this book to you. It was because of a challenge created by an inspired nugget from God. I actually challenged Him on the merit of the words because I failed *to see* the implicit inspiration. Admittedly, I did not find immediate inspiration in a particular nugget of wisdom about death.

"Why is it that we view death so painfully when it appears to afford the dead such peace?"

GMT #2710

I felt betrayed and setup by God with this nugget. It was difficult to believe I could honestly speak to it. I believed that to do so would place me in a position of hypocrisy. You see, I had taken the inspired words literally and failed to ask God for clarification. I voiced my anger to Him and decided to step away from it all to include my relationship with Him. I did not sever the relationship completely, but I put some distance between us. I didn't talk to Him as much nor did I talk about Him to others, as I had in the past. The time away from God allowed me to consider my issue with Him. The nugget that caused disappointment was about the pain that death causes and the peace it seemingly affords the dead.

Certainly, I accepted the essence of death, except I had seen the peace it spoke of in the faces of my deceased loved ones, but not in my husband, Robert. His death was tragic and horrific. The fire consumed aircraft that carried he and two hundred and forty seven other soldiers only left charred remains. The exception was Robert's body was at best intact. The Army assured me the remains released to me were Robert, but I was not comfortable with their assurances. I therefore allowed four of our closest friends, all male; to view his remains for my peace of mind. The wait for their kind selfless labor was unbearable, as with each second I questioned my decision not to view him myself. Can you see where this is going? First, I decided not to view him. I then believed God had given me an inspiration about seeing him. Whew! I watched each man's face appearing as if he had tried to give Robert back a portion of life for the sake of dignity. Their faces were all soaked with tears, as they too had lost a dear friend. I nonetheless went to each one and asked, "Did you see Robert, and was it him? Please don't lie to me, did you see Robert?" One by one they nodded and said, "Yes, it was Robert." I can't imagine what they saw, but I now know the nugget God gave me was as much for them as it was for me. Still I asked, how could God ask me to inspire anyone with such words?

My compromised relationship with God grew heavy on my heart and I begged Him to forgive me. However, I did not ask for forgiveness because of clarity. I asked for forgiveness because I missed God in my daily life. I had grown to depend on Him and talked to Him as you would any dearest friend. I missed it dearly. It was as if He was waiting for me to ask Him. God resumed my inspirational nuggets, as He too had stopped talking to me. A couple of months later I asked Him to reveal the wisdom in the nugget He obviously intended me to deliver. He led me to examine the nugget more closely. The points of clarification were very simple. I robbed myself of seeing them by focusing selfishly.

- **Point One:** Death is painful.
- **Point Two:** Our view of death and not the physical body controls our spiritual resolve.
- **Point Three:** The initial peace afforded the dead is not determined by their death, but by their life.
- **Point Five:** The peace the dead experience is between their God and them.
- **Point Five:** The spirit of life left by them despite death determines the peace left to loved ones.
- **Point Six:** Supremely, the spirit of the dead is given a chance to live through the lives it touched...

The clarification gave wings to my spiritual resolve and helped me *to see* the peace for Robert and peace of mind for me. The inspiring nugget moved from being my least favorite to one of my cherished. Death is about how to live life more abundantly. Did that resolve lessen my pain of loss? No, it just made it lovingly bearable. The nugget of wisdom, though from unlikely means found space in my spirit that wisdom feeds often. It actually taught me how to fish for more. Can you see it? If not, don't stop looking, for there are nuggets of wisdom from every inspired word.

In the end, I learned motivation and inspiration helps God to weigh our spirit. That is to say, how much of Him we harvest daily. You already know that I do not believe we can pass any of His tests. As such, He lovingly let's us step on His scales. He has shown me that we can increase our weight by using motivation and inspiration as He intended.

You must find a way to use motivation with expectations of inspiration. Your decision to do otherwise is a recipe for defeat. Inspiration must become a driving force from within. I am an advocate for power and strength coming from within, so let's explore that perspective one more time. I want you to experience victory, so expect flashing lights to signal your spirit that inspiration is coming. I make no assumptions about your understanding, which is why I step away and give you examples. Here are a few examples of power from within. Clearly, man extracted knowledge from things already in existence and all other discoveries were all borne of them.

•Man's physical power is ignited by food and water — taken within
•Man's intellectual power is ignited by thinking — taken within
••Automobile's power is fueled by gasoline — taken within
•Fuel that allows airplanes to soar — taken within

Can you see it? Something must be taken within before power is outwardly revealed. It does not matter if it is man, beast or machine. No power in, no power out. *Whew!*

Motivation and inspiration are good fuel for your spirit. Don't fail by separating them. Allow them within and pray for wisdom to convert them into the power you will need to exercise universal spirituality. There are several short Actions items for you before I release you. Use your responses for growth.

ACTION: What is motivation to you?

____

____

____

ACTION: What is inspiration to you?

____

____

____

ACTION: Can you *see* how motivation and inspiration can work better as a team?
Yes_____ No_____

ACTION: Let your Get Me Thru Partner know if you intend to partner with inspiration and motivation henceforth.

ACTION: Develop a system of accountability with your Get Me Thru Partner. I am not going to provide you a guide for this Action, because I want you to create it together.

ACTION: Secure your book and prepare to perform each exercise now as honestly as possible. My wager is on you just for having come this far. Don't ever let this book get dusty. Use it on days when you can't see yourself and especially after you do ...

I shall continue to work daily on my spiritual strength and weight. I pray you too learn how to increase your spiritual weight as you step on the scales of spirituality in life. Please let me know if you gained any weight through these exercises.

A Get Me Thru Nugget:

"No Comparing,
No Complaining,
but
Setting a Standard..."

HAIL MARY CHAPTER

The Coach Steps Away...

Coaches spend a lot of time with their players. They also spend a lot of time alone planning what to say to their players. The quietness normally screams the loudest in their hearts after the team is gone. This is that time for me. I am now left with my thoughts. Did I get the words right? Did I prepare you for victory? Did I give you enough of me? Did I make a difference for you? These are questions I am certain every Coach, whether in athletics or in life has also asked. I assure you I listened to **The Voice of My Boundaries** throughout my revelations to you.

Nevertheless, I want to put a Hail Mary Pass into play before penning my final words to you. Football enthusiasts know it to be a pass thrown very high into the air giving all players in place an opportunity to catch it. Certainly, Coaches pray that one of their players makes the catch. I am not selfish, because I want everyone who reads my book to catch the pass. Here's the pass. I am just going to walk around and talk to you in *nuggets of wisdom*. There will be no episodes, no Actions, just nuggets that I hope you catch and use to run all the way to your goals and dreams.

- Be careful of jealousy and envy of what others have, for you have no true way of knowing how they got it, nor what they are doing to keep it.

- Trust your *Inner Voic*e to guide you to action and you won't have to suffer your *conscience* reminding you that you did not listen.

- Set achievable goals when you begin *to practice* new perspectives and build confidence for the more challenging goals to come.

- Tomorrow can stand as a witness to your excuses or as a character reference and partner to your spiritual resolve.

- When you fail to think for yourself there is always someone else willing to think for you. The problem is —you may never know the difference for sure...

- Everyone was born to make a difference while on this earth. Divinely, life represents *Truth* revealed by the *Light* that individuals radiate through faith.

- Exercise your weaknesses, not just because they are where they are, but because they can keep you there...

- Your blessings are not withheld from you, they are in you from birth just waiting to be released as you travel through your journey.

- Know God for yourself, but also enjoy experiencing Him through the lives of others.

On that note, I will bid you farewell…

Venita

The Get Me Thru Coach